Untold Dairies

The Pages that Bled

KREESHA THANKI

BlueRose ONE.com
Stories Matter
NewDelhi • London

BLUEROSE PUBLISHERS
India | U.K.

BlueRose ONE.com
Stories Matter
NewDelhi • London

For permissions requests or inquiries regarding this publication, please contact:

BLUEROSE PUBLISHERS
www.BlueRoseONE.com
info@bluerosepublishers.com
+91 8882 898 898
+4407342408967

ISBN: 978-93-7139-122-1

Cover design: Yash Singhal
Typesetting: Namrata Saini

First Edition: July 2025

Trust me when I say for every person home is not their comfort, for some people home is the reason for escape." Every individual of every age and every relation has the right to choose their own life. Every person in this world should feel free to build their lives with their choice. No matter how external factor influences your life, it matters to satisfy your inner self in the end.

Hello, this is Kreesha just an 18-year-old girl, on a way for others to consider me as an adult.... oh! Let me make it clear, not since I started my adolescence but before even, I was of 10. Of course, living in a brown Indian family being a girl clearly defines how I should be. So basically attractive, calm, sincere, intelligent, non-dramatic and shy. Although I would agree my family to be better than few others around me, they could be better.

Sometimes I have to think of my parents and our surroundings because they play a crucial way in my life. "Because my life is more of them than mine"

OK! Let me clarify this is not just my feelings but sentiments and emotions of 75% of offspring in India. Being a child in India is more difficult than having one's seat in parliament.

It makes me sad but, even after living in a democratic country the youngsters of the house have to go through a strong dictatorship. It's not just about freedom or happiness but it is more about understanding, knowing, sacrificing and much more...

But although they always end with "What problem do you have in your Life? We provide you with the best life...."

I never said, but I have to because parents now have to understand that even being a child in the family is difficult. Probably not in every family but in most. I won't blame but I strongly expect every parent to understand these views from a child's perspective.

A person gets their personality developed from their environment. And for a child, their primitive environment is their home, with their family. The way parents will behave with their child will be given back by that child to others after becoming an adult. Core values and moral values of the child are developed by the high influence of parents. This book is not based on philosophy, for proper evidence and reason I have tried my best to reach most cases through interviews or case studies.

Just us listening,

"you kids have no idea how difficult it is being a parent or maybe you won't understand our sacrifice or worries towards you.... Damm! Do you have any idea about your future? You're not at all serious towards your goal or you have no goal., look at your cousin they are the same as your age but better than you, you don't know how terrible the world is, and much more"

To be honest, every child values their parents' concern and sentiments but,

Parents have no idea sometimes that it is even difficult to be a child, Mumma pappa do you understand the sacrifice and worries we have about you?

From habits to securing your future, the thousands of sacrifices that a child makes for their parents are unfortunately not valued. "It's ok I'll become a doctor papa won't agree, no worries I'll manage being in the same city, I'll compromise towards my choice of partner, aren't these sacrifices? And do parents still think their kids don't think of them, they don't know about the world.?"

Yes, we are glad that our parents worry about us, yes, we agree that even many times we are wrong, and yes, we do agree that maybe we are not perfect, but in the end, we are too humans.

If you are a parent, you know but maybe you don't your actions and emotions towards your child are responsible for their overall self attributes.

A child develops their self-esteem between the ages of 6 to 7 if they have grown up through positive regard of parenting, they will have strong positive self-esteem and if negative parenting towards them then they might develop low self-esteem but, unfortunately, no one is ready to understand the basic knowing's for a child's development and instead they are been treated to the basses of their parents' mood.

I love my country but to be very honest, my country needs to realize that your parenting is not just going to affect your child's future but even the upcoming future of our country. I won't teach about parenting coz I am not a parent but being a child, I hold infect every child holds the thought to be understood, known and emotionally supported and if you are a parent, I wish you to understand...

And here is the diary of knowing your child....

And not just parents....

The actual game starts from the society...

Sometimes it's not fate or failure that breaks a person – it's society. It starts with the comparisons that turn confidence into self-doubt.

A child who is full of dreams is told they're not enough because they don't score as high, look a certain way, or fit into a perfect mould. Slowly, that child becomes a teenager who hides their true self, who's afraid to speak, afraid to feel, because society only accepts what they understand – and they understand very little.

They're told to chase jobs, not passions; to marry for status, not love; to stay silent, not strong. Emotions are mocked, mistakes are broadcasted, and healing is never offered – only judgment. People begin to live for others, not themselves, and in that process, their identity fades. Society teaches you how to exist – but not how to live.

And that's how it ruins someone, not in one moment, but piece by piece until they're just a shadow of who they were meant to be.

Our family or parents can be simply considered a part of our society. Later they usually act as puppets of society. Maybe that's not their fault, but no one took a major initiative to change this theme, and it is continued.

Being in an Eastern culture our personality is highly influenced and controlled by the culture and society.

Well, society never realizes the pain that they are passing on to the future generation. The constant fear of following the norms of society becomes traumatizing.

Our society never realizes but, but

Our society often silently kills the actual self of a person by demanding perfection, performance, and polished masks over authenticity.

From a very young age, individuals are taught to measure worth through their achievements, appearances, and productivity rather than inner peace, empathy, or connection.

Emotions are seen as weakness, sensitivity is mocked, and asking for help is treated as failure.

People are told to be independent to the point of isolation, to compete even with loved ones, and to keep smiling even when their souls are tired.

Identity becomes a product that is shaped by the brands, trends, and careers–until a person forgets what their actual self is before they are told who to be.

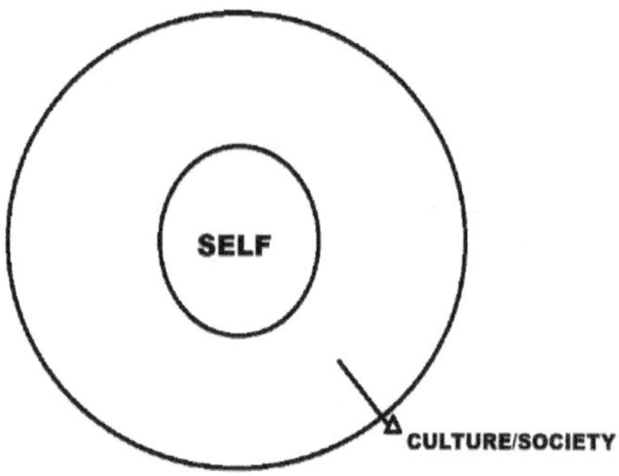

but they never did" I don't know but it does not make sense to me when I get ten to twelve calls from my house within an hour when I was not at home...I don't feel that is care it clearly shows trust issues towards me...I just needed a break...and no more allegations. It sounds ok but it is difficult.

"There is a difference between showing care and doubting."

Dear parent,

Don't be a red flag to your child, because it always ends with trust.

Dear of an unknown

12th November

Dear Diary,

My family hates it when I go out of home, although they allow me but still in the back of their mind they do not like. And I know it clearly so I don't prefer regularly to go out of my home but at least I deserve one a week, no matter where I am, or even if I am out for my work, I have to get back to the house at 7 pm, literally when people start their outing, I end mine. Anyway, yesterday a few of my friends requested me to join dinner with them and...with high hash!

I agreed to their plan. And I had to leave dinner in between because my parents thought that maybe I was smoking somewhere, having drugs or I was somewhere alone with some guy. Although I was with my friends and one of their family. And I left dinner out there in between. I was home at 7:16 just sixteen minutes later than my border time. My parents acted to me as if I did a crime and I was back home....no it was just bloody sixteen minutes. I never wanted to show my parents bad in front of my friends but they had an obsession with showing their actual side to my mates what could I do that? My parents asked me who was the guy you were with.... I wish I could say my life has other things to do except a guy. "People will say their daughter has no manners that she gets back home so late" It was 7:16 not even 8. And if they want me to hold society of my head, I wish I was never born...this was not the only case but whenever I go out, I move with fear in my mind. But I have to go out to get some peace because my peace is always broken with my own parents...

I can't find peace within my house, so I try to find shadows out of my house, but they every time break the shadow and ruin like a heavy sun ray.

I wish for many things but it always ends with their wish.

Sometimes it feels like they had a better life because,

On a slow night when they played with their friends in the streets, I ended up crying alone in my room.

When they share incidents with friends, I am quiet because I have nothing to say.

They had a group of friends, that I never got a chance to get.

"No, I don't search for freedom, I pray for peace."

We agree we are not perfect; we agree we are not the kids that you want we agree we are not like you, but from our parents, we never expect a lack of trust, we need time to say that "when the world won't trust me, my parents will" no your child is not a Lier, you can trust them and if sometimes a lie goes out it has no intentions to harm anyone in the most of the cases it is your fear in our minds.

In the end, expectations are kept from our people, and everyone knows that no one can be so bad except our parents, dear parents if you won't trust your child, then this world won't trust them.

In the end, we want it from you, and yes, if you think that there is always earning in trust, "a parent never needs a reason for loving their child, and trust is a major pillar of love." If you say that you love your child come on say that you also trust your child.

Usually, parents expect their children to share every moment happening in their life, but there is a big "what if" What if my parent won't trust me after this, every relationship in this world.

We really love our parents, and even our parents do but mostly they don't trust...believe me, we want to speak the truth, but because you don't trust us, we have to be a cap.

"You want us to be the prisoners in a prison working hard but, we won't be a traveller, travelling the world and knowing different people" If you trust us, we can turn out to be our best and beyond your expectations.

If you trust your child you'll know them beneath, if you trust your child, you will know the trust and finally your child will be able to feel at home in you.

Darling your child needs your trust, they won't say you but they crave your trust. Because trust is fundamental to a healthy parent-child relationship that fosters emotional connections and comfort of truth.

For a child, it is never easy to live in a family that has no trust in them. It feels so similar to a relationship that has no bounds of trust. Lack of trust in a family towards teenagers can negatively impact a child's development, potentially leading to difficulties and emotional and overall well-being. No one knows or agrees but it is difficult...

expectations but never acceptance

"We are expected to be silent, we are expected to be the pride of our family, but we are never accepted for what we are." When my parents told me, we have hopes in you to achieve your goal, many times I wanted to

Whisper in their ears that you were expecting that I wouldn't to able to accept. You want me to live in your ways, and when I shouted against it you were never ready to accept that to your child you are more like a warden and less like a parent.

I strongly feel parenting is not about instructing, it is more about understanding. It is not about give and take it is all selfless. And when you start accepting and not expecting it turns true and pure.

And even if you expect it, accept it and admit that you expected it.

It might turn harsh to parents but many of them don't accept and that attitude of not accepting develops an attitude even for the child of not accepting so in future your child won't accept what they had to.

When parents tell their child, no we didn't mean that, we didn't say you doing that, I never scolded you, we have never made you cry or we have never done bad to you, yes you did that but unintentionally.

I never know if is that an excuse for not accepting or if you didn't, because that many times gives us trauma. And you'll know now...

"Many things are unknown, similarly many reasons are not accepted."

Dairy of a fourteen-year unknown girl.

19th September

Dear Diary,

My father thinks he is the best father in this world, yes but he was best for me until I realized what wrong was happening with me. No living in a brown family is not living in an average normal family. It is beyond bizarre, difficult to understand and a problem with no clue.

Yes, I want to be their pride, but not to be society's bride, how it feels when you look around and its expectations, expectations and expectations, how it feels one would know when your own don't accept you. Hah! I live in India my parents are not accepting me so I have no expectations that my in-laws will accept me in future. Because being a happy and bold girl in India is never accepted by society.

And yes, no more I can stay happy for long because they feel weird when I dance happy so for their acceptance, I have stopped expecting happy acts for myself now...kudos to them because their expectations won't allow me someday to accept myself. Being the elder daughter of my family, I have always been expected and never accepted. Since the age of ten, I was expected to do every household but I was never accepted for my mistakes, I am always expected to be perfect but never accepted when I am imperfect.

My life went like a seesaw between expectations and goals towards fulfilling their expectations, and the moment I missed or failed on their expectations seesaw got imbalanced. And that is the reason for my mental imbalance. Yes of course I love my parents but I cannot adore or love them for this. If really, they wanted their child to live only for their expectations I wish they could better choose to invest in human Robert.

I love them but with intense fear. To be honest I am tired. And I can't push myself anymore. But the show won't end because ultimately, I am brick of their free...

So, wish me luck.

They don't say sometimes but their acts do, I am expected to take care of the house and do household, I am expected to get good marks for society, I am expected to be silent, I am expected to wear what they want me to, I am accepted to make a goal of their choice in my life because I am expected to be like a robot and not a human.

And so, I don't expect from life because I have started accepting but,

I am not bold anymore, I turned silent.

I don't speak more because they don't expect me to...

I breathe but not with my open arms.

Diary of some unknown,

Diary of an unknown 21-year-old girl.

Dear diary, 2nd February

Tired of Expectations, Starving for Acceptance

Today I woke up feeling heavy. Not because of the world,

but because of the weight others have placed on me.

They don't see me. They see what they want from me.

A version they've created.

A puppet they pull strings on.

A name without a story.

A smile without struggle.

I'm tired.

Tired of trying to fit into frames that were never shaped for me.

Tired of being told who I should be – louder, quieter, tougher, softer, smarter, simpler, more this, less that.

When will just "me" be enough?

No one asks,

"What do you want?"

"Are you okay?"

They only speak in expectations, not empathy.

They clap when I perform, but leave when I fall.

Some days, I just want someone to sit beside me in silence

and not try to fix me –

Just accept me.

Not because I'm useful, impressive, or convenient –

But because I exist.

But maybe that's too much to ask in a world that's addicted to performance

and allergic to authenticity.

So, I stay in the unknown. Quiet. Misunderstood. A whisper in a room full of noise.

Not because I have nothing to say –

But because I'm done screaming just to be heard. Maybe one day, someone will look at me and not see a checklist...

but a person.

Until then, I write here.

Where I can finally be... real.

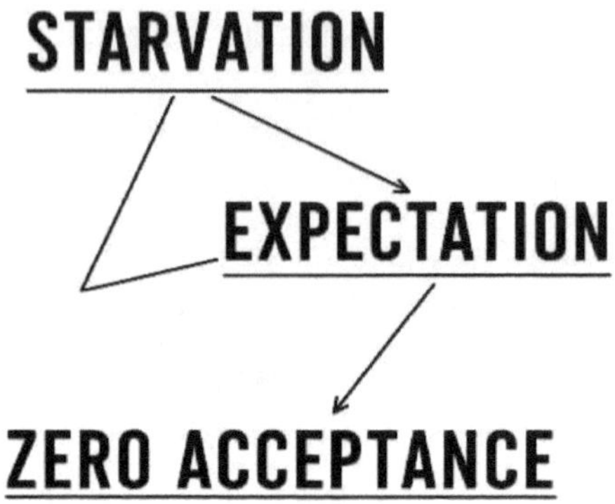

"Sometimes story ends because of the expectations because storyteller knows that story was never going to get acceptance."

Not just one dairy, but this dairy is connected to thousands of stories it ends the story and starts new,

People, family, society always wants us to follow their expectations but than latter it ends with zero acceptance.

With a lot of sympathy, though if a person wants empathy they do not get.

Dairy of 18-year-old

Dear Dairy

12th September

You know my name,

You know my age,

You know me,

Yes, you know my abilities but always focus on my disabilities.

Of course, you know my talent which always gets fed under the competition of grades.

They know my mistakes but they never know me.

Literally every day I wake up wearing myself that I didn't choose just to be what they want me to be...well, I smile a lot while I am hurting myself from every corner of my heart and brain.

I'm the child of a checklist –

✓ get the grades that they want.

✓ Don't talk back

✓ Make them proud

✓ Don't feel too much

✓ fulfilling their dreams that they couldn't do.

✓ following the rules of society

Sometimes, I think I'm not their child.

Just a reflection of everything they couldn't be.

To me, it's more suffocating. And now I have started feeling myself in a cage of expectations, orders, millions of conditions...

Sometimes I get scared thinking of what if I failed what they want me to be and because of this my nights and equal to my days....

Unknown 18-year-old girl dairy

Dear diary, 12th October

With a heavy heart, torn eye, speechless tongue and overthinking mind. I am tired actually more than tired, now I have turned hopeless and lifeless....

Freedom?

It's a word I write in my diary, not something I live.

Because the world around me...

They want discipline, not difference.

Silence, not self-expression.

Obedience, not originality.

Yes, I live in a democratic country of freedom, but unfortunately, I cannot enjoy my freedom because I am my parent's and relatives' property.

I feel 0 I feel more like a Robert and less like a human, because I have to do what they want me to do, because I have to act the way they want me to act, I have to choose the career that they saw for me and yes mainly what is triggering me is that I am not a human with freedom clearly, I am a living human in an invisible cage.

"Dear society for me freedom is not late-night parties, for me freedom is not drinking and smoking, for me freedom is not wearing reading, but for me, freedom is sitting quite in a garden alone or maybe with my few friends,

freedom is exploring places and people, for me, freedom

is not taking permission for even going to a shop just 2 meters away from my house. "

Parents are not enough to restrict me it starts from...

Society says,

"Follow the norm."

"Dress this way."

"Act that way."

"Don't talk too loud."

"Don't feel too much."

"Don't be different."

And yes, sometimes I hate myself for being a girl because again society says...

"don't wear so short"

"don't talk with boys"

"don't make boyfriends"

"Oh, you are not a good girl you go out late at night"

Dear society I'll shut my brain now because my brain cells are forced to work the way you want me to, why should I waste the energy of my brain than....

I was not born to be another ID tag in a dusty drawer.

I was born to live, to breathe, to scream, to dance in chaos and to find my own meaning.

This is the diary of someone society never tried to free.

Of someone who stopped asking for permission –And started asking why No offence, but I hate society,

Diary of an unknown 19-year-old girl

Dear diary,

8th December

This morning I went for a short walk around the corner of my area, my eye got stuck looking at a man painting on a canvas, with his messy hands covered with different paints and his face with sweat. But, a part of this all I saw a happiness on his face I don't know for what reason but, he had a short smile and a rose of satisfaction in his eyes.

I went to him and asked, "For how much you are selling this small canvas painting?" for a second, he looked at me than his painting again and then at his painting and replied to me with a smile "For 120 rupees madam" I agreed to buy that canvas painting.

Ahm! Not because that painting attracted me but, because I could see myself instead of that man.

Since childhood, I was extremely fervent and sure about choosing painting and being an artist in my career.

In my schools, I was known for making good paintings. My room had hundreds of paintings on walls, doors, and windows everywhere you look in my room there were just paintings.

And I was pretty sure that if that became my profession, I would reach to the high heights of it. But unfortunately, that was not my destiny.

My parents and a few relatives gave me a denial for that profession. Few people told me,

"That profession is not for girls"

Some of my relatives manipulated my parents by saying,

"After some age, she has to move to her in-laws and this profession will keep her busy for a whole day this will create massive issues in her in-law's family."

And can you believe one of the aunts who said this to my parents, her daughter who is almost two years older than me is one of the best painters in our city she gets paid in lakhs for her paintings. And this hurts me more...

Today I could have been one of the best painters in our city or maybe country instead of wasting time in an engineering college.

Anyway, I brought that paint to my home and kept it to my study table which is totally opposite to my bed every night when I sleep, I will look at that painting and remember about my art that was never allowed to bloom...

I just hope that someday I will start painting with that same dedication.

Maybe one day, I'll pick up the brush again.

Maybe one day, I'll let the world watch me paint.

And not care if they clap.

But for now... I remain

A painter in silence.

An unknown in a world that doesn't recognize me.

Dairy of an 11-year-boy

Dear dairy

12th march

Today, I danced again.

But only when the door was locked.

Only when mummy was in the kitchen and papa was not home.

I don't know all the steps, but my heart does.

My heart tells me where my legs have to move and where my hands have to curve,

I was enjoying the moment of dancing and going lalala... with my mood. While dancing I was thinking of my school dance teacher praising me for my every little dance moves.

I continued my dance for almost 2 long hours. Yes, my happiness had no end but I had a corner of sadness in my heart because I knew my parents never wanted me to dance, my parents could not afford me to dance.

My mother was looking at me from the kitchen continuously, I thought that she would scold me but unexpectedly she dint said me anything.

I was enjoying every beat and step of dance; those lyrics were going through every muscle that moved effortlessly.

I was literally dreaming of being one of the best dancers in my country, and somewhere from the corner of my heart.

I knew that my dream of being a dancer wouldn't get fulfilled maybe...

But yesterday, when Papa saw me copying a classical dancer on TV,

He turned it off.

He didn't tell me anything.

His silence was loud.

It made me feel like I did something against him...

At dinner, he told Mummy,

"Why is he doing all this girly stuff?

"Take his admission in some football or cricket academy."

I just kept eating without a word, my spoon was shaking and my eyes had tiers but they were not allowed to move out...

Because I was scared of listening, "now! Don't cry like a girl, for this small matter."

I hope I can dance someday with all my open arms in front of the world.

One day, I hope someone like me reads the dances with the door open. Until then, I will dance in silence, and smile in secret.

Dairy of a 12-year-old girl

Dear diary,

9th June

I don't speak much anymore.

Not because I can't.

But because the world doesn't listen.

They say I'm too quiet, too reserved, too strange.

But what they don't know is – I've seen too much.

Heard too many lies dressed as concern.

Watched people perform kindness for applause, not care.

In a world obsessed with being heard,

I became invisible on purpose.

Not as an act of weakness – but of resistance.

They want noise.

I give them silence.

They want an explanation.

I give them a mystery.

Sometimes I sit on a bus and stare out the window,

Watching people glued to their screens –

Texting, scrolling, and pretending to connect while running from themselves.

Nobody looks up.

Nobody notices me.

And that's the best part.

Because in this quiet,

I hear things most people miss –

The tremble in someone's voice when they say "I'm fine."

The way a smile fades the moment no one's looking.

The tired eyes behind a perfect selfie.

I'm not lost.

I'm just not interested in being found by a world

That claps for loud lies and mocks quiet truths.

Sometimes I want to scream,

Not out of pain, but to shatter the performance.

To remind them that the quiet ones are not empty –

We are full. Overfull.

Of thoughts.

Of stories.

Of truths too raw to be spoken out loud.

One day, I'll speak.

But not for approval.

Not to be liked.

Only to tell a story that will burn through all the noise like wildfire.

Until then,

Let them call me silent.

Let them think I'm unknown

That's where I'm safest.

That's where I'm most real.

Dairy of an 18-year-old girl

Dear Dairy 3rd April

Sometimes I feel like I was born with wings but in a cage.

I gave an audition for a TV series last month. The result came out today and surprisingly I was selected for the main character of that serial.

That moment looking out myself selected for the main character took my breath and my mouth open. I was damm so happy that I literally wanted to shout out loud and tell this news to my family, relatives and literally every person in my street.

But I thought to wait until the right time arrived.

I waited for about 2 days and on Friday when we were having lunch in our garden,

I decided to pinch the point without fear. And I said "pa pa, papa I am sorry" but for what my father asked and my brain got blank. I replied with an intense fear of rejection about the audition. And as expected my father replied,

Acting is not for our family and we do not allow our girls to get into that career. Papaa please I got selected for the main character, listen girl I won't allow you for any reason and the discussion ends here.

I knew this was going to happen, but still, I had hope that ended within seconds.

Well, when I gave the latter of denial to the casting team,

My eyes were with sorrow,

My hands were not ready to write the letter of denial.

My heart got high beats

And I turned silent.

All I wish now is to get my own freedom in some other era of mine.

And if not me I wish for the freedom to every other person to take a chance of their opportunity.

Dairy of a 17-year-old boy

Dear Dairy 10th April

I'm 17. And I'm exhausted.

Not from studies. Not from sports. Not from staying up late.

But from pretending... from existing in a world that never seems to listen.

Every person around me, my parents, my uncle, my aunt literally every person has decided what I have to do.

Everyone is expecting and wants me to do the things that they have planned for you, yes, they are doing without my preference of knowing.

Yes, they wanted me to become a builder but they never focused on my skills of singing.

Yes, people want me to be strong so, they always ignore my emotions.

Everyone wants something from me.

Be better. Study harder. Don't cry. Don't talk back. Be strong.

Be a "man".

But I'm just a kid trying to figure out who I am.

I don’t even know what I like anymore. I used to love solving cubes. Now I haven’t touched my cube in months.

The society I live in has already decided the version of me it wants:

Silent. Obedient. "Successful".

But no one asked what I wanted.

Sometimes I just want to scream. But I’ve mastered the art of smiling instead.

Because crying is a "weakness" and I’m not allowed that luxury, am I?

I see people post fake happiness online, while I delete messages, I wrote but never sent.

Because who would care if I said,

"I’m not okay."

And even if they will show some care, how can I trust them I am sorry, but in case I don’t want to make my life problems someone’s gossip.

Every time I try to speak my truth, someone shuts the door with,

"Don't overthink."

"You’ll be fine."

"It's just a phase."

But what if it’s not?

All I want is a place where I can be real.

Where I can just breathe without being judged.

Where I can say,

"I'm struggling."

And hear back,

"It's okay. I'm here."

Until then, I’ll keep writing in these pages.

Because paper doesn’t interrupt.

It just listens.

Dear dairy **I don't remember,**

I remember it was weekends. My aunt came to our home. I never said but I literally hate not just her but her whole family. And the reason is very obvious to me that her whole family thinks that they are mostly right and we are bloody uneducated although we hold more education than her family.

She literally started telling my mom that she should focus on me and get me into the households and yes just a common dialogue from Indian society "Jidhar jayegi udhar se vapis ayegi" My mother is literally a sensitive person she gets affected if someone tells her even a silly thing.

I really know,

That aunt does not care about me,

I know she just wants to be the best Front of others...

That aunt started telling my other that her kids are so punctual and dedicated. And dear dairy you will know further about their dedication.

Because she told my mother to focus on me, my mother came to me at night and said you have to be better, look at her kids the way they are, look at their discipline, and learn from her daughter she is so into households and her son he is so struggling and sure about his work. You have to learn from them. The aunt told me you are not on the right path...

Come on show me your phone now, I know you are dating someone...

What! Seriously Mumma, just because she thought that I am not proper you are doubting me...but, that ok take my phone check if you get anything.

A few weeks later I got the news that her daughter was up to get a divorce because her husband did not agree with her thought of living separate from his parents and everyone among our relatives was convincing her to change her decision.... I am sorry I don't mind that is her personal choice, but then where was her mother at that time....?

And her son did physically abuse her cousin's sister...

I am sorry but, I was right I never wanted to learn anything from them...

I am happy for I am...

I know to be a better person...

And literally, I don't care anymore for others' opinions.

Dairy of a 17-year-old girl

Dear diary, 5th October

Time: 9:00 PM

Dear Diary,

Today felt heavy again. I don't know why I try so hard to fit in when it feels like I'll never truly belong. The kids in the neighbourhood were playing outside again – laughing, shouting, being... normal. I stood by the window for a while, wondering what it would be like to be part of that. But when I walk near them, it's like I turn invisible.

I tried saying hi to Rohan, but he just nodded and kept talking to the others. I even helped his little brother last week when he fell off his bike. I thought maybe that counted for something. I guess not.

At school, it's the same story. Everyone has their own group, their own inside jokes, their own little world. And I'm always watching from outside, pretending it doesn't hurt.

I tell myself it's okay. Maybe one day, someone will see me – really see me – and not just pass me by like I'm background noise.

I'm tired of being the "quiet one," the "strange kid," or worse – the one nobody remembers at all.

But for now, I have you, dear diary. At least here, I exist.

Good night.

As an introvert maybe, people don't choose us or simply ignores us. back of our mind that triggers a lot.

Here's a short poem that felt my heart...

No, they can see me,
Infect I am clearly visible,
But than its their choice to ignore me.

I was always with them.
And they threw me to the bin.
I feel it's okay,
But that is hard to know.

Under every shadow,
I am fool alone.
Under every dark,
I am alone to clone.

And to every person,
I'll try to be their own

Dairy of a 15-year-old teenager

Dear Diary, 2nd December

Sometimes I wonder... when did the world become so cruel? Or maybe it was always this way, and I just didn't notice until now.

Everywhere I turn, people are judging. For how you look, how you speak, what you wear, what you believe – even for just being yourself. It's like society is built to break people down, not lift them up.

They tell us to be "real," but then they criticize every honest thing we say. They tell us to be strong but give us no space to cry. They say "You're too young to understand," yet expect us to carry the weight of expectations like adults.

Why is it so hard for people to be kind? A simple smile, a kind word, or just not being cruel – is that too much to ask? I see people getting mocked online, bullied in school, ignored at home... and all anyone says is, "That's just life." But why does life have to be this way?

I've learned to keep quiet. To stay in the background. To pretend I'm fine when I'm not. Because if you show weakness, they tear you apart. If you show strength, they try to bring you down. Either way, it's never enough.

I wish the world understood that we're all fighting battles they can't see. I wish people knew that words leave scars deeper than they realize.

Maybe one day, things will change. But tonight, I just feel tired.

Thanks for listening, diary. At least here, I can speak freely.

– A Tired Teen

Dairy of 12-year-old girl

Dear dairy 8th march

I am already tired of bloody black spots on my face. I literally had the clearest face before few months...and now suddenly my face has black spots and they look me so ugly. My mind constantly thinks about those scares, my heart feels heavy now, and I am literally dealing hard these days.

I am sure, If I tell this problem to other people they will act as if they care but I know they don't, I know only a few who actually care.

Well, last Saturday my mother and I went to the dermatologist for a checkup on what was actually going wrong and after the doctor took a workshop, he said that I was facing a disease named 'lichen planus' and that was a psychosomatic disorder, that affects your immune system and latter your melanoma production in the skin. "Okay doctor but when will I get relief from these li, li lichen planus? It is already getting so suffocating for me to live with this spot..." dear I am sorry but these black spots generally do not mark their absence and if it does it takes a long time maybe 6 to 8 years...

We came home, and I turned quiet...

I turned quiet for ten days then fifteen and then for a month...

Every people asked me in different ways...

"Heyy!! What's wrong with your face?"

"I think you eat so much junk looks at your face what happened?"

"Why has your face turned so dull?"

And of course, these questions were not enough what traumatized me emotionally and mentally was...

"Omg! You have started looking so ugly"

"You do not look so attractive"

"Your era of being beautiful has finally ended..."

And, the gem of society

"With these scares on your face, it is difficult for us to find a man for you"

I was already disturbed mentally and people pushed it more......that forced me to silence and I stopped going out, I ignored the family gatherings, friends' meet-ups and all other gatherings...

Because I knew my scars would get more deeper than healing...

And I know,

Society is never kind.

Dairy of some unknown

Dear Dairy 9th August

Good evening, it’s my birthday and it's 8 pm now. When I was a child, I loved my birthdays. My mother and father lived in Dubai. On my every birthday, my father made sure to make it as as special he could. My birthdays were like festivals for my parents.

They started preparing for 9th August every time before a week. And all mornings of my birthday were supper sweet. My father wakes at 5 in the morning that day and he decorate the whole house like a palace before I wake up, he makes delicious deserts for me and starts my day. Now when I remember that being a child, I have enjoyed every birthday...and now the story has turned different I just wish that my birthday skips...

In 2013 we shifted back to India. And started living in a joint family of 9 members. I don’t know why but my aunt hates me. And she ensures to make my every day the worst one. Yes, of course, she shows herself to be the most kind and helpful woman for me the back stories are never known...

Since 2013, I have not celebrated those sweet birthdays again. On my every birthday now, I have they make me realize that for them my birth was a curse... and I really don’t know why, but my father does not make the same efforts he made before...

I know the reason, but...

I know if he will make the effort for my birthdays. She will start sharing her views with a fight that they have not celebrated any birthdays for her kids why my birthday...

But that was their choice for not celebrating their birthdays no one forced them not to celebrate...and at least their birthdays are not considered a curse like mine.

Being a child, I was always waiting curiously for how my birthday would turn floral and now, before every birthday I pray that no more dramas bring out on that day. Now I don't cut the cakes, I don't expect gifts or surprises all I know and expect is the traumas.

I remember 2 years on my birthday, my mother was secretly planning for my birthday and a few of my rebel family members created a huge fight just because my mother decided to make some efforts for my birthday.

The fight went so crazy that most people in our house cried and that day I saw my mother's heart broken into pieces, my dad's eyes with sorrow and guilt.

I feel sorry for them, I know I am a curse but, I can't see guilt and pain in them...

I hope to never see my birthdays again...

I hope this was my last birthday.

I hope for happiness in their eyes when their curse might die. And, I am really sorry to them.

Another year, another day
But joy seems far and away...
No more cheers and candles in the corner,

All I can see is chaos on that day.
No birthday songs, no one to sing.
Just memories like faded art,
And wishes carved in aching heart.

They say with age, we learn to grow,
But not all wounds are meant to show.
Sometimes the smile hides the pain—
A birthday spent alone... again.
No more, I wish my birthdays again...

But still, a whisper in the night,
Reminds me stars outlive the light.
So, I'll make a wish, not loud, just true,
That someday joy will find me too.

Dairy of a 13-year-old girl

Dear dairy Date: The day I lost parts of me

It was just a normal classroom.

A teacher asked a question about depression. I raised my hand – said I think mental health should be treated the same as physical illness. Sometimes, people smile but are dying inside.

The class laughed. Someone whispered,

"Why are you always so dramatic?"

Another said,

"Maybe you should see a doctor if you're that messed up."

I laughed with them.

Pretended it was funny.

But my hands were shaking under the desk.

Because the truth was...

I had tried to take my own life three weeks before that day.

I didn't tell anyone. Not my friends. Not my parents.

Because I didn't want them to look at me like I was broken.

But that moment – that laughter – hit me harder than any pain I'd felt before.

Because if I had told them the truth,

If I had said, "I swallowed 8 pills and stared at the ceiling, hoping not to wake up"

Would they still laugh?

Would they still think I was "too much"?

Society teaches you to hide.

To shrink.

To shut your mouth and just "be normal."

But I don't know what normal feels like anymore.

Is it normal to cry in the shower so no one hears?

To keep telling yourself, "I'm fine" when everything inside you is screaming?

To feel like a burden when all you wanted was to be understood?

That day changed me.

Not because I realized I was different.

But because I finally understood:

Society doesn't hate the pain – it hates it when you show it.

It hates the raw. The real. The unfiltered truth.

So, I learned to wear a mask.

Perfect marks. Polite smiles.

But inside, I was slowly dying.

I'm still here.

Not because I'm strong.

But because deep down, there's a small voice that whispers:

"One day, your truth will help someone else survive."

Until then, I'll keep writing.

Even if no one reads this.

Dairy of some unknown

11th January

Dear Diary,

Things are not the same as it was, I don't remember the last time I laughed without fear of something going wrong with me, I don't remember the last time I trusted someone, and I don't remember myself as I was before.

I feel hidden now, I feel more useless now it seems as if I am the worst. I remember about joy. It has been almost four years today. Four years since everything has changed. I have seen the hurdles of mine that changed me whole a person.

There were the days that I danced so hard that the audience could not stop clapping, there were the days when I walked so gracefully that the judges gave me a standing ovation, and there were the days when I was one of the prettiest girls in our blood.

I gave an audition for a beauty pageant, and just like every time I was selected, I went for the 20-day competition with my mother and I was just fourteen. For a few days, I rocked every stage, every single day. On the 18th day of the pageant competition, one of the choreographers physically harassed me. , I really didn't know how I could react, I didn't know what was happening...my eyes couldn't view anything, my mind went blank and I could do nothing...anyhow I escaped and went to my mother

I wanted to tell my mother everything that happened but I wasn't able to tell her, I was scared. That night of course wasn't able to sleep anyhow I just wanted to leave that place and get back home.

I started acting as my health so getting worse...and requested my mother to get back home. And on the next day, we went home in the evening. I was having a hush about being home. Until...

My cousin's brother had come to our place just to spend his vacation who was twenty-two years old. We were so close but then he did the same physical harassment... and he said "You're so pretty even I deserve" and that voice shrinks my ears to the date.

Since then,

I started hating myself, I stopped dancing and modelling, I stopped trusting people,

And now,

Not anymore, I am an extrovert;

I get scared while connecting with people......

That has changed me as a whole.......

Dairy of a girl

Dear dairy

9:30 pm

Place: School gate, under a sky that never cared

It happened so fast.

I was standing outside the school, waiting for my auto. I had just laughed at something my friend said – one of those rare laughs that feels honest, open, loud.

That's when I noticed him.

A man. Phone in hand.

Pointed right at me.

Click.

At first, I thought I imagined it.

But no.

He smirked.

He walked away casually as if he had just captured something he owned. I froze.

I wanted to scream.

I wanted to run and grab his phone.

But instead... I stood still.

Like a statue.

Like prey.

My friend asked what happened.

I said, “Nothing.”

Because I didn’t want her to panic.

Because deep down, I already knew:

It didn’t matter.

By evening, my mind had built a hundred stories.

What if he uploads it?

What if someone uses it?

What if it reaches people I know?

What if the angle was wrong?

What if my laugh – that one moment of joy – becomes my shame?

I told my mom.

She said,

“Next time, don’t stand alone.”

It was my fault for being visible.

Dairy of a 14-year-old girl.

Dear Diary,

Date: 14th August – the day I stopped looking in the mirror

Place: A crowded wedding hall filled with "well-wishers"

They say Indian weddings are full of color, music, and celebration.

But for me, that night felt like standing naked in front of a firing squad –

except their weapons were smiles, and their bullets were comments.

I had worn a lehenga I loved.

It was soft, and pastel, with little mirrors that caught the light.

For once, I felt... okay. Not perfect. Not stunning. Just okay in my skin.

I thought maybe this time, I wouldn't be judged.

I was wrong.

“Areey beta, you’ve put on some weight, haven’t you?”

“Girls your age should start walking in the morning.”

“That lehenga is a bit tight, right?”

“Who will marry her if she stays like this?”

Each sentence was wrapped in sugar but pierced like knives.

They smiled while saying it.

Like I should be grateful for their concern.

And the worst part?

My mom laughed.

My aunt nodded.

Even I… smiled.

Because I didn’t want them to see how much it hurt.

That night, I came home and stood in front of the mirror.

I pinched the fat on my arms.

Stared at my stomach.

Pulled my cheeks back.

And whispered,

"Why are you like this?"

That was the night I stopped wearing what I loved.

I started layering clothes to hide every inch of me.

I skipped meals.

I Googled "how to lose weight fast" more than I Googled anything else.

Society doesn't even realize what it does.

They think body shaming is advice.

They think they're helping.

But what they do is plant seeds of hatred –

not for them, but for ourselves.

Now I fear every family function.

Every festival.

Every mirror.

Every camera.

Not because I don't love my body...But because I've been taught others don't.

Dairy of 20-year-old

Dear Diary, 7th July

I want to heal.

I want to wear yellow again without wondering if it makes me look "fatter."

Sometimes, I want to get well dressed but I cannot, just because I have the fear of people judging me...

"She is so fat, why is she wearing such dress?"

Yes, I know that I am fat...

Yes, I know I cannot wear every type of cloth,

But I don't know, why people take so much interest in my dressing.

On my last weekend, I went for an outing with my friends...when I was coming back my neighbour Aunty said oh where is Miss Universe coming from? And I said simply that I went for an outing with my friends, and she said okay! But why are you wearing a dress, you know you are oversized right? And dear that does not suit you.

I don't know why, but now I don't feel like wearing dresses.

And that is not enough. Sometimes I feel that being fat is like a mistake that I made. People often tell me ways of losing weight. But I cannot because I have a thyroid that puts on my weight. And I have to accept my weight.

No, drinking hot water with lemon won't reduce my weight. I have to take my medications and wait until the miracle happens. And this same thing I said to a few of my relatives when they were showing me fake concern regarding me, that I won't find any man because I am overweight...

And no not just a few of my relatives but seriously many and many relatives I guess almost 47 people from my society, friends and neighbors showed me this fake concern, and most bitter about this is that they then gossip about my weight in front of me for hours.

And yes, when I try to explain my weight to them or the actual reason behind it...usually people argue that you are just giving an excuse.

"don't eat junk" ....

No, I am not eating any junk food. I take my proper healthy diet. Yes, I do eat junk but once a month and just 20% of the total portion.

"Do proper exercise"

I walk 1200 steps daily...

Wherever I go people just end up on my weight.

And now I am tired of knowing in a hundred ways from others that I am fat.

Yes, I know that I am fat but I don't want any validation....

And I am now tired of knowing that I am fat and I should be within my limits now need someone to understand and know me without any judgments.

I don't want people to judge me anymore, and let me do what I want.

I want to dance without feeling my body jiggle and wondering who's watching.

I want to look in the mirror and say, "You are enough" – and believe it.

But for now,

I hide behind oversized hoodies, fake smiles, and this diary.

Maybe that’s where healing begins –

in writing what I can't say aloud. – A girl who didn’t need to be fixed – just accepted

Diary of an unknown

Dear Diary,

You know right? That I live in a toxic family?

They say family is supposed to be your safe place – but mine feels like a battlefield dressed as a home. Everything here is loud: the shouting, the slamming doors, the constant blaming. And yet, somehow, the silence hurts more. The kind of silence when I cry in my room and no one asks why.

The kind where my feelings are dismissed as "drama" and my voice is treated like a threat. I walk on eggshells here. One wrong word, one misunderstood tone, and suddenly I'm the villain. The ungrateful child. The burden.

Love here comes with conditions. I have to act happy to be accepted. I have to agree with everything to avoid conflict. If I say how I feel, I'm "disrespectful." If I cry, I'm "too sensitive." If I get angry, I'm just like "them."

I don't remember the last time I felt seen without being judged or compared. Every little achievement is ignored, but every mistake is magnified like a spotlight on my flaws. I don't remember the last time my parents hugged me. I'm not allowed to break down, yet I'm expected to hold everything together. For them. Always for them.

Sometimes, I wonder – if I disappeared, would they miss me? Or would they just miss having someone to blame?

This house is not a home.

It's a place where my smile is forced and my silence is survival.

Dairy of a teenager

Dear Diary,

Today, I woke up with that heavy feeling again—the one that wraps around my chest like a chain and whispers, "You're not enough." I didn't even want to get out of bed. Not because I was lazy, but because the thought of facing the world felt like going into battle... unarmed.

Why is it like this?

Why does society act like being a teenager is a crime?

We're either too loud or too quiet, too bold or too shy, too skinny or too fat, too modern or too backward. It's like no matter what we do, we're never "just right." We're judged for the clothes we wear, the music we like, the dreams we chase. If a boy cries, he's weak. If a girl speaks up, she's "too much." If you try to be different, they laugh. If you try to fit in, they still find flaws.

I'm tired of adults calling us "the future" but never letting us be human in the present.

I once heard someone say, "Teenagers are just drama." But has anyone ever stopped to ask why we're this emotional? Maybe it's because we're drowning in expectations. Maybe it's because we're trying to find ourselves while the world is constantly telling us who to be.

Social media is worse. Everyone's smiling, posing, living their "best life." And here I am, feeling like a mess for not having clear skin, a perfect body, or a thousand followers. It's like being in a race I never signed up for.

Sometimes, I wish I could scream. Not for attention, but for freedom—freedom from judgment, from gossip, from society's labels.

They say we're too young to understand the world. But maybe it's the world that refuses to understand us.

Anyway, I'm exhausted.

Just wanted to let it out. Maybe tomorrow will be better... or maybe I'll just get better at pretending.

Love,

Dairy of some unknown

Dear Diary,

Dear past me,

Found your old diary today – the pages smudged with dried tears; the words heavy with pain. I read your entries like they were echoes from a haunted house I once lived in.

You were so tired. So desperate to be seen without being judged. You let them shape you like clay, breaking your edges just to fit their shallow shelves. They told you who to be – slim, smart, quiet, obedient, invisible – and you believed them. Even when it hurt.

Do you remember that day you wore something you loved and they called it "too much"? Or when you laughed loudly and someone told you to "act decent"? You began to shrink after that. And every time you did, they called it maturity.

But now, I'm writing to you from a world where I've unlearned their voices.

Here, no one cares if your jeans are ripped or your accent is different. Here, dreams don't come with warnings. You are allowed to cry, to fail, to heal – without hiding.

But I want to say thank you.

Because even when you were drowning, you held your breath for me.

You wrote down your pain so I could remember what to never become again.

You stayed alive in a world that kept telling you not to exist too loudly.

And that... is brave.

So, this diary – your diary – won't end in sadness. It ends with freedom.

Not just from society... but from the guilt of being yourself.

I promise I'll carry you gently now.

You've earned your rest.

She wasn't broken by the world outside,

But by the walls where she was told to hide.

A house that fakes, a house that she lies, the walls between she cried in, and the tiers that she hid...

They said words that broke but never held her hand,
They called her weak but didn't understand.
She carried storms in a quiet soul,
While pretending that she was whole.

In a place where she was never allowed to choose.
Her laughter became a forgotten sound,

She cried in corners no one would see,
Begging, "Why can't my family just love me for me?"
They mocked her tears, called her ungrateful,
Yet drank from her spirit till it was hateful.

She begged for warmth, received cold blame,
They loved her only when she felt shame.
They remembered her only when needed.
And so, she broke – not with a scream,
But with silence sharper than any dream.

Now she walks like a ghost in her skin,
A girl who lost before life could begin.
Just with the hope that some spark survives.

Dear Dairy 2nd February

Today, I woke up with a weight on my chest. Not the kind of sleep fixes – the kind society builds with bricks of judgment, cemented with expectations.

I'm tired.

Tired of pretending.

Tired of smiling when I want to scream.

Tired of shrinking myself to fit into their little boxes of "normal," "successful," and "respectable."

They don't ask if I'm okay.

They ask:

"What's next?"

"Why haven't you achieved this yet?"

"When will you be like them?"

When I try to speak, they label me as weak, lazy, and too sensitive.

But they never see the battles I fight in silence – the wars between my mind and the masks I'm forced to wear.

I walk through a world where everyone is performing – and I'm exhausted from playing a part I never auditioned for.

I live in a society that tells and shouts at me to go ahead and then stops me pointing a gun. It is difficult to be.

Why is it that being different is treated like a disease?

Why is rest mistaken for failure?

Why is honesty seen as rebellion?

I'm not broken. I'm just tired.

Tired of running a race I never signed up for.

Tired of chasing a version of myself that society painted for me.

Tired of existing instead of living.

They have hundreds of questions to me, they have thousands of doubts on me, they want me to be silence may be a nest in a silent tree.

I know I am not perfect,

I know I am not so as them...

But I also know what I have they don't maybe manners...

Maybe one day, I'll find a place where I can just be.

Not perfect. Not polished. Just... real.

But until then, I'll keep breathing. Quietly. Softly. On my terms.

Because even if society doesn't get it, I know I'm trying.

And that should be enough.

Dairy of a girl,

Dear Diary,

Today, I walked out of my therapist's clinic feeling a little lighter – not healed, not fixed but heard. Just heard. And that's something I don't get out here.

But the moment I stepped out, and came near my streets the aunties there disturbed me again, they were discussing as if I was unstable...

"She's in therapy? Must be mentally unstable."

"He must've gone mad, poor thing."

"As if therapy helps – just attention-seeking."

They say it all. Quietly, loudly. Some say it behind my back, others just directly enough to cut.

Let me make this clear, just once:

I go to therapy because I want to get better – not because I'm broken beyond repair.

I speak to a professional because my mind deserves as much care as a fevered body or a broken leg.

I cry in those sessions because it's the only space where I'm not judged.

But society? It makes me want to shut up and shrink.

They call it "drama" if I express emotion.

They say "You're overthinking" when I share my pain.

They say "Just be positive" like it's a magic pill.

I'm not weak. I'm surviving in a world that teaches us to stay silent until we shatter.

Why is seeking help considered shameful?

Why is being in pain such a threat to their version of "normal"? Although I think that those gossiping about someone's health are abnormal or unstable not me...

If anything, therapy has taught me to face myself. To heal, not hide.

It's a society that's still sick – still afraid of honesty, still allergic to emotion.

But I refuse to be silent anymore.

I will talk. I will heal. I will grow.

And maybe one day, therapy won't be whispered about like a dirty secret – but spoken of as a sign of strength.

Until then, I will keep going. One session, one step, one breath at a time.

I know how easily society can break a person. These people broke the hidden peace of mine. And I am suffering hard today.

- The One They Called "Unstable"

Diary of a Teenager

Dear dairy, Date: The 365th day of pretending

Today, I smiled again when they asked if I had a "crush on any girl."

I laughed it off. Like always. Like it's a joke I never wrote but am forced to perform.

But inside? I'm drowning in silence.

I've known who I am for a long time.

I didn't "turn" this way.

I didn't "choose" a different path.

I just am – like anyone else. Except the world doesn't see me that way.

Every day, I wear a mask. Not for fashion.

But for survival.

Because if I speak –

I risk being hated by my family.

I risk losing friends who preach love but draw the line at people like me.

I risk being called disgusting, confused, broken.

And so, I stay silent.

I bite my tongue when someone says "It's just a phase."

I nod when they say "You'll find the right opposite gender someday."

I sit through casual slurs like it's just background noise.

But this silence?
It isn't peaceful.
It's loud. It's heavy. It's exhausting.

I want to love freely.
I want to walk without hiding.
I want to be seen – truly seen – without fear.

Because my love is not a crime.
My identity is not shameful.
And I am not a secret.

Maybe one day, I'll speak my truth out loud –
Not just on pages no one reads,
But in a world that finally listens without hate.

Until then, this diary is the only place where I exist without apology.

- Someone Still in the Closet, but Not Broken

Dear dairy

Today, I sat quietly while my classmates talked about their vacation plans – hill stations, resorts, shopping sprees.

I nodded. Smiled. Pretended I could relate.

But my mind wandered back home – to a leaking roof, to skipped meals, to my mother working late shifts just so I could attend this school.

I'm tired.

Not just physically, but in ways that no sleep can fix.

Tired of hiding the same shoes I wear every day.

Tired of pretending I forgot my lunch when I didn't have anything to bring.

Tired of hearing, "You probably won't get it," whenever something costs money I don't have.

They don't say it outright. But their looks, their words, their pity – it speaks louder than anything.

They assume I'm lazy.

They assume I don't dream big.

They assume I'm "used to less."

But they don't see the hunger behind my eyes – not just for food, but for a chance.

A chance to be more than my wallet.

A chance to be seen for my heart, my effort, my worth.

Why does society measure respect by bank balance?

Why do they ignore the ones who struggle the most?

I didn't choose this life.

But I'm not ashamed of it either.

I know what it means to value things.

To fight for every small victory.

To rise without a cushion to fall back on.

And one day, when I make it –

Not just for me, but for my family –

I won't forget what this felt like.

Because I wasn't poor in dreams.

Just ignored by a world too rich in judgment.

- The One They Chose Not to See

Dairy of a young girl.

Dear dairy

Today, I opened my phone and fell into the usual trap.

She got into her dream college.

He's starting a business at 17.

They just hit 1 million followers.

And me?

I'm just here. Breathing. Barely.

I didn't even get out of bed till noon today.

And when I did, I stared into the mirror, wondering what was wrong with me.

Why am I not like them?

Everyone online seems to have it figured out – perfect bodies, perfect relationships, perfect achievements.

Every swipe reminds me of what I don't have.

And society doesn't help either.

"At your age, we were already doing this..."

"Look at your cousin – she's already making her parents proud."

Proud.

That's a word I haven't heard in a while.

It's like my worth is measured in likes, ranks, and results.

As if existing isn't enough anymore.

No one sees the pressure. The anxiety. The self-doubt that social media quietly feeds us.

It's a comparison trap that looks pretty – but feels like drowning.

I'm tired of chasing someone else's highlight reel.

Tired of pretending I'm okay with being "behind."

Tired of thinking I'm not enough.

But deep down...

I know life isn't a race.

I know not everyone's success looks the same.

And I know I have time. Even if the world tells me otherwise.

So, for tonight, I'll put the phone away.

And just let myself be.

Flawed. Human. Healing.

And maybe, just maybe... that's enough.

Today, I finally told someone I wasn't okay.

And guess what they said?

"Just stay positive."

As if those two words are some kinds of magic spell that fixes everything.

But they don't know.

They don't see the nights I cry myself to sleep.

They don't hear the thoughts that scream in my head.

They don't feel the heaviness in my chest when I try to smile for everyone else's comfort.

I'm tired.

Not just of the pain – but of being dismissed.

Every time I try to speak, I'm told:

"Be grateful."

"Other people have it worse."

"Don't be so negative."

But what about me?

Am I not allowed to feel what I'm going through?

This isn't about being negative.

It's about being human.

Positivity isn't always the answer. Sometimes, all we need is someone to listen.

To say, "I hear you. I believe you. I'm here."

But instead, they hand me empty sunshine while I drown in my storm.

I'm not weak.

I'm not dramatic.

I'm just tired of pretending everything's fine when it's not.

So tonight, I let myself cry.

Not because I'm giving up –

But because I refuse to keep pretending that everything is okay when it isn't.

And that... is also a strength.

Dairy of some unknown

Dear Dairy 8th September

I stared at my reflection for 10 minutes today.

Not in admiration – but in quiet frustration.

Picking apart my skin. My shape. My scars. My so-called "flaws."

Wondering why I can't look like them.

You know – the ones on Instagram.

Flawless skin. Perfect waist. Sculpted face. Glossy smiles.

The kind of beauty the world claps for, double-taps for.

And me?

I turn my camera on and instantly feel like I need a filter to exist.

Every post, every story, every comment whispers the same lie:

"You're not enough unless you look like this."

I try to dress up.

I try the diets.

I suck in my stomach in pictures.

I tilt my face just right.

And still... I don't feel beautiful.

Society doesn't just want me to be healthy –

It wants me to shrink, to soften, to vanish into its impossible ideals.

To be thin, but not too thin.

To be curvy, but not too curvy.

It is natural, but only if it still looks like perfection.

I'm tired.

Tired of hating the body that carries me.

Tired of scrolling through lives edited beyond reality.

Tired of thinking I'm less because I don't look like a photoshopped fantasy.

But tonight, I whispered something new to myself:

"I am not a filter. I am not a trend. I am not a mistake."

I may not be everyone's version of beautiful.

But this body has survived every single day – even the cruel ones.

And that's worth loving.

Dairy of a girl,

Dear dairy some unknown day

Today I want to write something for my younger self...

Dear Younger Me,

I wish I could hold you – not to fix you, but to hear you.

To tell you, "You never had to carry it all alone."

I remember how you tried to fit in... how you folded yourself into smaller shapes just to be accepted.

How you laughed when you wanted to cry.

How you stayed silent about your fears, your pain, your truth – because society made it feel unsafe to be real.

They told you to "toughen up."

To "act normal."

To "stop being dramatic."

But what they never asked was, "Are you okay?"

And you weren't.

You were hurting.

You were confused.

You were tired – not from being weak, but from being ignored.

Whether it was the weight of hiding who you were...

The shame they made you feel for your body, your trauma, your emotions...

Or the pain of growing up in a world that judged your silence more than the reasons behind it...

You carried it all – and you still found a way to survive.

I see now how brave you were.

It takes so much strength to wake up every day in a world that doesn't see you, and still try to live.

So here I am, years later, writing this with love in every word:

You didn't break.

You bloomed in places no one thought possible.

The world never made it easy – but you made it through.

And not just by surviving – by slowly, quietly, beautifully becoming yourself.

You will unlearn the shame.

You will outgrow the fear.

You will find people who love you not despite your story, but because of it.

So, if you're reading this from your darkest corner,

Just know:

Your light never left you – it was just waiting to be seen.

And one day...

You'll be everything they said you couldn't be – and more.

With pride,

Your Future Self – whole, healing, and finally free

June 22, 2025,

Dear Diary,

I don't even know where to start tonight. I feel like I'm carrying the weight of expectations that were never even mine to begin with. Every day, it's the same cycle – wake up, get scolded for something, go through the day pretending I'm okay, and then cry myself to sleep.

It's not that I hate my parents. I love them. But I'm tired. Tired of not being heard. Tired of feeling like I'm never enough – not smart enough, not obedient enough, not the version of me they imagined when I was born.

They don't understand that I'm a person too, not just their daughter. I have thoughts, feelings, and dreams that aren't always the same as theirs. But to them, my opinions are either "disrespectful" or "too dramatic." How is wanting to be myself a rebellion?

Sometimes I wonder what it would be like to just... be free. To wake up and not be judged for the clothes I wear, the music I listen to, or the way I talk. I want to breathe without feeling like I'm doing something wrong.

I know they care. Maybe they're just scared – scared of the world, scared of me making mistakes. But I wish they knew that controlling everything isn't love. It's suffocating.

Tonight, I'm writing this not out of anger, but exhaustion. I just want a little peace – a little understanding. Is that too much to ask?

Yours,

A Girl Who Just Wants to Be Heard

Would you like a version in poetic form or from a younger or older girl's perspective?

Unknown dairy

Dear Diary, 22nd June

I never thought I'd be writing about this.

About her.

The friend I trusted with everything – my secrets, my silence, my loudest laughs, and even my insecurities.

She wasn't just a friend. She was like a sister.

We did everything together. Shared snacks, shared crushes, shared dreams. I believed her when she said, "I've got your back."

But today I realized... she had a knife behind it the whole time.

I don't know what hurt more – her betrayal or the fact that she didn't even feel guilty. She talked about me behind my back, twisted my words, and told people things I trusted her with. And the worst part? She smiled at me like nothing happened.

Was I that blind? Or just that loyal?

I keep replaying everything in my head – every joke we shared, every hug, every late-night call – and now it all feels fake.

I keep asking myself:

What did I do wrong?

Why wasn't I enough as a friend?

But maybe the truth is, some people don't change. They just reveal who they are when they think you're not looking.

I won't cry over her anymore. I've wasted enough tears.

From now on, I'm going to be smarter with who I trust.

It hurts – God, it hurts – but maybe it's better to know the truth than live in a lie.

Goodbye, old friend.

Hello, new me.

Yours truly,

A Girl Who Deserved Better

Would you like me to turn this into a story or a poem next?

"She Was My Friend"

A Girl Who Deserved Better

She knew my laugh, she knew my pain,
We danced in the sunshine and cried in the rain.
She held my hand through every fall,
Or so I thought – she faked it all.
A whisper here, a twisted lie,
Behind my back, while meeting my eye.

She stole my trust with gentle grace,
Then broke my heart – without a trace.
The secrets I gave, the truths I shared,
She wore them like weapons and never cared.

A smile so sweet, a voice so kind,
But poison hid behind her mind.
I called her sister, I called her soul,

But she was playing a darker role.
Now silence sits where laughter grew,
The girl I knew – I never knew.

No final words, no sorry said,
Just the ghost of friendship, cold and dead.
Yet through this ...

Dairy that was never told…

June 22, 2025,

Dear Diary,

I can't stop shaking.

Not because I'm cold, but because the world we live in is so cruel… so unfair… so wrong.

She was my best friend. She still is. But now, she's not the same. Not because of what happened – that monster took something from her, yes – but because of what society did after.

They didn't protect her.

They didn't believe her.

They blamed her.

"What was she wearing?"

"Why was she out so late?"

"Are you sure it wasn't just a misunderstanding?"

I've heard these words a hundred times this week. Not from strangers – from aunties, uncles, teachers, even people who smiled at her once. The same mouths that praised her for being "such a good girl" are now using words like attention seeker, drama queen, and shameless.

Shameless?

The only one who should be ashamed is the one who hurt her.

But instead, she's the one hiding in her room, eyes swollen, voice silent, heart shattered.

And me? I sit here, filled with rage, helplessness, and guilt. Guilt because I don't know how to help her. Because I watched people talk and didn't scream. Because I see her disappearing a little more every day.

She didn't deserve this.

She deserved support, love, justice.

But this society gave her stares, whispers, and silence.

If she ever reads this, I hope she knows:

I believe her.

I'll stand by her.

And I will never let this world turn its back on her again.

She is not what happened to her.

She is still strong. Still pure. Still my best friend.

Forever,

A Girl Who Will Never Be Silent Again

Dairy of silence,

June 22, 2025

Dear Diary,

Why does it feel like no matter what we do, it's never good enough for society?

If you speak your truth, they say you're too loud.

If you stay silent, they say you're weak.

If you wear what you like, you're "asking for attention."

If you cover up, you're "too boring."

I'm so tired of living in a world that always finds something wrong with who I am.

Tired of being told to smile more.

Tired of being judged for the way I talk, walk, sit, dream, and live.

Tired of a society that wants to control girls like puppets but takes no responsibility when we break.

They talk about values, culture, and respect – but only when it suits them.

They blame victims, mock the brave, and glorify the fake.

If you fall, they laugh.

If you rise, they try to pull you down.

If something bad happens to you, they ask, "What did you do wrong?"

Sometimes, I wonder if society even has a heart.

Does it ever stop to think before pointing fingers?

Does it know the damage it causes with its toxic words and outdated rules?

I wish, just for once, society could be kind.

Not perfect – just human.

Empathetic. Understanding.

Fair.

But maybe that's asking for too much.

Still, I'll continue to live my truth.

Even if the world keeps shouting at me – I'll keep walking.

Because I'd rather be hated for who I am than loved for a lie.

Yours,

A Girl Who Sees Through Society's Mask

Would you like a poem or spoken word version of this?

Some unknown dairy

Dear dairy

They asked me why I was always so quiet.

Why I never joined the laughter.

Why I never brought friends home.

Why do I stop speaking up in class?

They never asked me what hurt me.

It was last year—when I gathered all my courage and told my parents I wanted to be a dancer.

Not an engineer.

Not a doctor.

Not what they wanted.

But what I dreamed of.

And my father didn't shout.

He laughed.

And then he said, "We didn't raise you for this shame."

That laughter haunts me more than any slap could.

The next day, my dance shoes were in the trash.

My mirror was covered.

And my dreams were declared "a phase."

It wasn't just my parents.

It was the aunties who whispered, "Too modern."

The uncles warned, "Who will marry her?"

The cousins who mocked me online.

And my friends—who went silent.

Do you know what it feels like to bury a dream while it's still breathing?

Now, I pretend.

Pretend to smile.

Pretend to be okay with a life someone else chose.

Pretend that the ache in my chest is just tiredness and not grief.

I sometimes dance in the dark when no one's home, just to remind myself I was once alive.

And I cry not because I'm weak.

I cried because I was strong enough to be honest—but that honesty was rejected like a disease.

This society doesn't kill dreams loudly.

It suffocates them, slowly.

Quietly.

Until you forget who you ever wanted to be.

Dear parent

I hope you read this with your heart, not just your eyes.

You always said you wanted the best for me.

But somehow, that always meant what you thought was best – not what I loved.

I told you I loved painting. You laughed.

I told you I wanted to be an artist. You called it a "hobby."

You said, "Engineering is secure. Respectable. Real."

You said, "Do this first, and later you can do whatever you want."

But what if this took everything from me?

Every day at that college, I felt like I was being buried alive.

Subjects I didn't understand.

Dreams I couldn't touch.

A world where I didn't belong.

I failed.

Not just the exams.

I failed at pretending.

At faking smiles.

At living a life that never felt like mine.

I stayed up every night, crying quietly under the blanket.

You thought I was sleeping.

You never noticed the red eyes.

The silence.

The fading smiles.

The boy you raised was breaking – and you kept pushing.

And I know you didn't mean to hurt me.

But Ma, Papa – you did.

You killed the artist in me first.

Then the human.

Now, only the shell remains – and I can't carry it anymore.

I'm tired.

Tired of disappointing you.

Tired of failing myself.

Tired of waking up to a future I don't want to live.

This is not your fault alone.

It's the weight of a world that worships marks more than mental health.

A society where dreams are dictated, not discovered.

I hope someday you'll understand – not just what I did, but why I did it.

And I hope you'll let my younger brother paint if he wants to.

Tell him... it's okay to choose happiness over expectation.

With love,

But no more strength,

– Your Son

Dairy of a teen,

Dear dairy

I don't know how to begin this entry without crying again.

But I guess… that's all I've been doing lately. Crying when I'm alone. Smiling when I'm not.

It's strange – how no one notices when you're falling apart.

I walk around this house like a shadow. My parents see my face every day, but I don't think they see me. Not really.

To them, I'm either the "good child" or the "disappointment" – depending on whether I meet their expectations that week.

An "A" means I'm their pride. A "B" means I'm a failure who wastes their sacrifices.

I tried telling Mom I've been feeling… off. My chest feels heavy, and some days I just want to disappear.

She told me to go to sleep early and stop watching sad movies.

Dad didn't even lift his eyes from his phone.

I wanted help.

I needed it.

But they made me feel guilty for struggling – as if pain needs permission to exist.

Every day, I wake up tired. Not because I didn't sleep, but because my soul was exhausted.

I try to breathe, but my lungs feel like they're full of water.

I try to focus, but my mind is loud – screaming lies I'm starting to believe.

"You're worthless."

"You'll never be good enough."

"They'd be better off without you."

I tried writing these thoughts in a letter once.

Then I burned it.

Because if they ever read it, they'd either mock me... or pity me. And I don't know which would hurt more.

Some nights I lie in bed and wonder what it would be like to just... not be here.

Not to die dramatically. Just to stop existing.

No more expectations. No more pressure. No more pretending.

But then I think of the few people who still smile at me – a friend who once told me, "You matter more than you know."

I don't fully believe it.

But I hold on to that sentence like a lifeline.

Because maybe... just maybe... someone out there will understand what I'm feeling.

Maybe this pain won't last forever.

Maybe one day I'll write a diary entry that ends with hope instead of hurt.

But for now –

I'm here.

Still breathing.

Still fighting.

And that, I guess, is something.

A young dairy..

Dear dairy

It happened in front of the entire school.

The whole damn school.

Morning assembly – the usual chaos, fake discipline, teachers shouting at latecomers, prefects acting like mini-principals. I was standing in the second row, trying to blend in, earbuds still buzzing with the last note of a song I didn't want to leave behind.

Then it started.

The whisper.

The shove.

The mocking laughs.

Some seniors were snickering behind me. I didn't think much at first – until one of them stepped forward and loudly said,

"Look at this guy. Is he wearing lip balm? Bro, are you gay or something?"

The word gay – is not even used as a label, just a weapon.

Suddenly all eyes turned.

Someone chuckled. Someone else whispered, "Yeah, he always looks too soft for a guy."

Another added, "Does he even play any sports? Probably writes poetry in his notebook."

I froze.

I couldn't speak. I couldn't move. I didn't know what the right reaction was.

Anger? Shame? Defence?

But I just stood there – my face burning, my throat dry.

Because if I lashed out, I'd be the "aggressive boy."

If I walked away, I'd be the "weak one."

So I stood there... dying inside.

When I got home, I washed my face three times. Scrubbed it until it turned red.

As if that would wash away the feeling of being less than.

What hurt more than the words was that not one teacher stopped it.

Not one friend stood by me.

Not even afterwards.

In school, boys can't be soft.

They can't wear lip balm.

They can't cry.

They can't be.

And God forbid if you're different – you'll be turned into a joke before you even realize it.

That day, I locked myself in my room.

I didn't eat.

I didn't cry.

I just stared at the wall and asked myself:

The common dairy,

Dear dairy

I didn't pass.

That's it.

Just a failed exam.

Not a crime.

Not the end of the world.

Not a reason to be treated like I was nothing.

But that's exactly how they made me feel – less than nothing.

The teacher called my name and threw my paper on the floor like trash.

She didn't just yell.

She slapped me.

Three times.

Once for each subject, I failed.

The whole class went silent – not out of sympathy, but fear.

No one stood up for me.

They just watched.

And when I thought it couldn't get worse, I went home.

And it did.

I walked in slowly, hoping maybe – just maybe – they'd ask if I was okay.

But before I could even speak, a shoe came flying.

Not one.

Two.

Papa's voice was louder than the pain in my body.

"You're useless. A shame to this family."

Mummy didn't stop him.

She just stood there and said,

"This is what we get for trusting you."

I wanted to scream,

"I tried."

But no one would listen.

I wanted to cry.

But they already decided that tears were a weakness.

So, I sat on the floor in silence.

Not because I had nothing to say –

but because they made me believe that my words, like my efforts, don't matter.

Do they even know how hard it was for me to hold it all together?

To try again and again when my mind was already drowning?

I may have failed in marks.

But they failed as my protectors.

As my family.

As my teachers.

Because education is supposed to lift you.

Do not break your spirit.

Right now, I don't feel like studying.

I don't feel like trying.

I don't feel like anything.

But I'm still here.

And that, for today, is enough.

Dairy of a girl

Dear dairy 12th may

They finally gave it a name.

Severe Clinical Depression.

Generalized Anxiety Disorder.

But society doesn't care about names.

They only care if you smile enough, dress "properly," and never talk too much – or too little.

They care about marks. No scars.

They care about beauty. Not bruises.

For years, I carried a weight I didn't understand.

It started small –

"You've gained weight."

"Why don't you talk more?"

"You'll never get married looking like that."

"Too ambitious. Too loud. Too opinionated."

"Don't laugh so much. Don't sit like that. Don't wear that."

Every word was a pin.

And eventually, I became a balloon full of holes – smiling on the outside, leaking silently from within.

I began skipping meals.

Avoiding mirrors.

Smiling for photos I hated being in.

Saying "I'm fine" even when I wanted to scream.

I stopped writing poetry.

I stopped looking people in the eye.

I stopped feeling like I was even here.

By the time I collapsed in the school bathroom with my heart racing and hands shaking, they still said, "She's just being dramatic."

Even after the diagnosis, someone said, "Everyone feels sad sometimes – just think positive."

Even after the medication, my relatives whispered, "Mental problems? What will people say?"

Society didn't see the girl who broke.

They only saw the girl who "failed" to meet their standards.

Now I sit here, writing this from a hospital bed – not for attention, but for relief.

Because finally, someone told me, "It's not your fault."

And I broke down.

Not from sadness – but because I'd waited my entire life to hear that.

This isn't the end.

But it's the start of reclaiming my voice – the one they tried to silence with shame.

If anyone ever reads this and feels the same –

Please know: It's not you. It's the noise outside you.

You are not weak for breaking.

You are strong for survival.

I wish I could say I don't care.

I wish I could say it doesn't hurt.

But today proved that no matter how hard I study, how well I behave, or how kindly I treat others – my last name will always speak louder than I do.

It happened during group project discussions.

We were supposed to form our teams – freedom to choose. Everyone picked their friends, naturally. I approached a group of four classmates I always helped with homework. I thought we were okay.

But one of them – Arjun – leaned in and said,

"Sorry bro, our group is full. Try the others."

I could tell he was lying. There were only four of them. Groups were allowed five. I stayed quiet. Moved to the next. Same excuse. Again. Again.

I stood alone in the corner as the teacher walked around, asking why I hadn't joined a group yet.

Then I heard it.

From behind me, whispered but loud enough:

"He's from that caste... you know. The reservation guys. Why should we take him?"

And someone else smirked and added:

"Exactly. They get everything handed to them anyway. Let them figure it out alone."

I stood there frozen.

It felt like someone had ripped my skin off and exposed something I never wanted to be judged.

How did they even know?

I've never said a word about my caste. Never used it to ask for favors. I've only ever worked twice as hard to prove I deserve to be here.

But today, none of that mattered.

I ended up in the "leftover group." The one formed by all the others no one picked.

Not because of our work. Not because of our attitude.

But because of our names, our skin tone, our silence.

When I got home, I wanted to scream.

But who would listen?

My parents would say, “Ignore them. Focus on your studies.”

But how long can you keep ignoring something that keeps following you everywhere?

I’m not angry that they didn’t choose me.

I’m angry that I was never even seen as equal, to begin with.

We talk about “New India,” about breaking barriers, about equality and youth and progress.

But in the eyes of society, I will still be less than – because my surname doesn’t carry power, or temples, or old money.

I didn’t choose this caste.

But today, this caste chose how the world would treat me.

Sometimes I wish I could erase it.

Start over.

Be “just a boy” – not a label, not a punchline, not a threat to their imagined superiority.

But all I can do now is write it here.

Because these pages don't care what caste I belong to.

They don't need me to prove my worth.

And maybe one day – when I have a voice louder than whispers – I'll write something bigger than this diary.

And people will finally listen.

Dairy that we know,

Dear Diary,

I heard the pressure cooker whistle from the kitchen today –

and for a second, my heart whispered, maybe it's calling me back.

Back to the space that made me feel alive.

Back to the only place I ever felt like me.

But then I opened my eyes –

and there it was, the thick, lifeless UPSC study guide on my desk.

A dream I never dreamt. A path I never picked. A future they decided for me.

You know, when I was 9, I made my first dish –

burnt toast with a slice of raw tomato and too much salt.

My mom laughed, and Dad ate it like it was gourmet.

Back then, I thought, this is love.

This is what I want to create for the rest of my life – something that brings people together.

But dreams, I've learned, are only respected when they sound "respectable."

And being a chef, to them, is just cooking in someone's kitchen.

They don't see the art.

They don't see the fire in my eyes when I chop, stir, taste, create.

They just say,

"It's not a real career."

"Become something prestigious."

"UPSC will give you power, status, and respect."

"No one marries a cook, beta."

And now, here I am –

18 years old, sitting in a room with walls covered in motivational quotes I didn't ask for.

Studying policies and polity, when all I want to do is learn plating and pastry science.

I tried telling them.

I begged once. Quietly.

"Please let me apply to culinary school."

Dad looked up from his newspaper and said,

"You want to wear an apron? After all, we invested in your education. You'll waste it all over spices?"

Mom didn't even look at me. Just said,

"Girls cook every day. That's not a profession, it's survival."

But they don't get it.

I don't want to cook for survival.

I want to cook for expression. For celebration. For soul.

Now I spend hours memorizing history I don't believe in, rules I don't care about,

while my notebooks fill with tiny doodles of kitchen knives and garnishes in the margins.

It's funny, isn't it?

The world tells us to follow our dreams –

But only if they're the dreams they approve of.

Sometimes, I sneak into the kitchen at 2 a.m.

When the house sleeps.

And I chop onions like they're the noise in my head.

Sauté my silence.

Season my sorrow.

And plate it all with a side of helplessness.

Every bite I cook alone feels like a letter to my future self –

saying, please don't forget who you are beneath all this forced ambition.

They think I'm preparing for UPSC.

But I'm preparing to leave –

to fight for the version of me that still believes it's not too late.

But until then, I write here.

Because at least in these pages, I'm still a girl who could've been a chef.

Dairy of some unknown

Dear Diary,

Nothing ended. Everything is the same, and I am here. Lately, I realized that hard incidents in your life don't end your life but unfortunately that changes you and your life completely. I live in a joint family which is the most difficult part of my life. I cannot blame my parents because my parenting is done by every elder in my house.

And they have authority over me. I feel sad and unhappy my heart flickers sometimes because authority is always misused. No, I am not considered to be the daughter of this house but a maid who works in regard to shelter and food. Ultimately, I have got more hatred and less love. My family hates me for no reason. And if they have a reason, I wish to know so that I can improve myself.

I want a family that knows to love I have dreamt and prayed for that which I never got.

Infect I have my biological parents who are not mine completely because they treat me the way their elders want. No, maybe it seems to be easy but that makes my daily life more difficult.

My every day is not chosen by my parents but by someone else, my choices are always compromised because we live in a joint family and yes what hurts me more is that my family remembers my existence at only two points...' when they want me to do some work or when they don't see me around. Well, every day in my life since I was 7 years old

some Incident that forced me to change myself. "I was born angel and my parents made me rebel..."

dairy that cried..

Dear Diary,

I didn't touch my pen today.

For the first time in years, the blank page didn't feel like a friend – it felt like a mirror,

reminding me of what I lost.

And I didn't lose a contest.

Or an opportunity.

I lost something worse.

I lost the one person who told me I could write... and then made me believe I shouldn't.

Her name is Anaya.

My best friend. My secret-keeper. My loudest cheerleader... or so I thought.

She used to read every poem I wrote.

Used to tell me, "You have something special. Don't stop."

She even cried once after reading a piece I wrote about my mom.

But everything changed the day my writing got selected for the inter-school magazine.

Suddenly, she wasn't clapping anymore.

Suddenly, my words became a competition.

"You write too emotionally. It's too much."

"Don't you think you're being too dramatic?"

"Nobody even reads stuff like this anymore."

"You're wasting your time. Focus on real things."

At first, I believed she was protecting me.

I thought maybe she was right – maybe I was being silly.

I stopped submitting my poems.

Stopped scribbling in the margins of my textbooks.

Stopped staying up late with ink on my fingers and stories in my head.

And every time I tried to write again; her voice echoed louder than my own:

"You're not that good."

But today...

Today, I opened my old notebook.

Pages filled with metaphors and scars and things I never said out loud.

And I saw it.

She wasn't protecting me.

She was afraid of me growing up without her.

She wanted me to stay small, quiet, ordinary – right next to her.

Because of my words? They scared her.

Not because they were bad,

but because they were true.

It hurts.

God, it hurts more than any rejection.

Because this wasn't from a stranger.

This was from someone who once told me she'd be the first to buy my book.

But now, I'm done letting her voice mute mine.

I'm taking my pen back.

Not because I'm confident.

Not because I don't still hear her doubts.

But because these words are mine.

And no friendship – no matter how familiar –

should cost me my voice.

So here I am, writing again.

My hand is shaky. My heart is heavy.

But this page?

This page is mine.

Dairy of a 14-year-old boy

Dear dairy

To whoever reads this,

I'm sorry.

Not because I want to be.

But because that's all I've been doing lately – apologizing for existing.

I failed.

Just one subject.

Math.

And yet, it feels like I failed as a son, a student, a human being.

The moment the results came out, everything changed.

Papa didn't say anything at first.

He just stared.

Like I'd stabbed him in the heart.

Then he said, "I had dreams for you."

Like I wasn't allowed to have any of my own.

Mom cried. Not the soft, worried kind of cry.

But the angry, ashamed one.

Like my failure was a stain on her motherhood.

She kept repeating, “What will people say? What will they think of us?”

Nobody asked me what I was thinking.

No one asked if I was okay.

No one asked if I wanted to try again.

The school didn’t help either.

My classmates laughed.

Some whispered, “How can someone fail in 10th? That’s the basics,”

And every word was like a stone tied to my chest.

But what hurts the most...

is that all this pressure wasn’t because I wasn’t capable.

It was because no one ever taught me that failing once is human.

Everyone told me to aim high –

but no one told me that falling doesn’t mean I’m not worthy of getting back up.

I’m not writing this to blame anyone.

I just want the world to know that your expectations crushed me.

Not my mistake.

Not the exam.

You.

You made me believe that I was only worthy if I succeeded.

You made me believe that my entire future was over because of one mark sheet.

You made me believe that love has conditions.

If only someone had said,

"It's okay."

"We'll try again."

"I'm proud of your effort."

But no one did.

And now it's too quiet.

And I'm too tired.

This isn't a goodbye with peace –

it's a goodbye with a heart that wants to live,

but was never taught how to survive failure.

To the next boy who fails in one subject:

I hope someone hugs you before it's too late.

I hope someone teaches you that a number doesn't decide your worth.

Because it didn't decide mine either.

But I just didn't know that... until now.

Dairy of a teen,

Dear dairy

Today was just like every other day...

Except today, it hurt a little more.

Today, I realized that in everyone's eyes – I am only as good as my report card.

It started at school.

We got back our unit test papers.

I failed. Again.

Not because I didn't try.

I stayed up the night before, trying to understand those math problems until the numbers started floating off the page.

But when I saw the red marks on my paper, I knew what was coming.

The teacher didn't say my name.

She said, "There are students in this class who are just wasting their parents' money."

And her eyes were on me.

The class laughed.

Some whispered, "He's dumbed anyway. Why is he even still here?"

And my so-called friends? They pretended not to know me.

At home, it got worse.

Papa didn't even ask if I was okay.

He just shouted:

"Why can't you be like your cousin? Look at him – always topping."

"Shameful. You have no future."

Mummy stayed silent.

That silence was louder than his shouting.

Even my little brother mocks me now.

Because he's already doing better than I did at his age.

And I'm just the example of "what not to become."

But no one sees me when I help in the kitchen.

Or when I fix the fan without being asked.

Or when I stay back to clean the classroom while others rush out laughing.

No one notices that I stay quiet, not because I don't care –

but because I'm scared.

Scared of failing.

Scared of being laughed at.

Scared of being reminded that in this world, being kind, being helpful, being me – is not enough.

They only want marks.

And if you can't give them that, they look right through you.

Sometimes, I wish they could read this diary.

Just once.

Maybe then they'd see that I'm trying – really trying.

Maybe then they'd stop comparing me to everyone else.

Maybe then they'd say something I've never heard before:

"You're not a failure. You're a fighter."

But until that day comes,

I'll keep writing here.

Because these pages are the only ones that listen without judging.

And for now... that's enough to keep me going.

Dairy of a 15-year-old girl

Dear Diary, 30th December

Today, I heard him laugh in the other room. Not with me. Never with me. Just like every other day.

It's funny how someone's voice can become the sound of pain instead of comfort.

I don't remember ever hearing my father say my name.

Not when I took my first steps.

Not when I scored the highest in class.

Not even when I fell sick and cried in bed for days.

Because I was never the son he wanted.

I was born wrong. That's what they made me believe.

Every time relatives came over; they praised my cousin's brothers.

"He's so smart." "He'll carry the family name."

And I? I became the shadow behind the curtain. A reminder of disappointment.

He talks to my brother like he's the only child.

They sit together, laugh together, eat together.

And I sit quietly with my plate, learning how to chew food and swallow feelings at the same time.

I've stopped trying to make him see me.

No more cards on Father's Day. No more waiting by the door for him to return from work.

Because the truth is–

He never left me. He never had me to begin with.

I didn't ask to be born.

I didn't ask to come as a girl.

But every day, I pay the price for being the "wrong gender" in a house that needed a boy.

Sometimes I wonder what it would feel like to be loved by your father.

To hear, "I'm proud of you."

To be hugged.

To just be... seen.

But until then, dear diary, I'll keep writing in these pages–

Because at least you don't stay silent.

– The Daughter He Never Spoke To

Dairy of a close one,

Dear Diary,

I held my cube in my hand today... not to solve it, but to say goodbye.

It wasn't just plastic to me. It was my peace. My pride. My place in this noisy, demanding world.

Each twist, each algorithm, each color falling into line – it gave me control when everything else in life felt like a mess.

I didn't pick up cubing because I had nothing better to do.

I picked it up because it made me feel something – seen, alive, talented.

And when I stood on that stage... when they announced my name at the national level, I thought for once– maybe they'd be proud.

But no.

"You waste so much time on this toy."

"Will this silly cube give you a job?"

"Stop acting smart, and go study like other boys."

They didn't even come to the award ceremony.

I had to take a selfie with the medal alone.

They made me pack away my cubes today.

Put them in a box. Lock them in the storeroom like some guilty secret.

As if passion is a shame and talent is a crime when it doesn't match their dreams.

I begged Diary. I did.

I told them it's more than a hobby – it's a skill, a sport, a future.

But all they saw was a distraction.

Do they know how it feels to be told that your proudest moment... meant nothing?

Do they know what it's like to be told that what you love has no value?

Maybe they never will.

Because they only see marks, degrees, and salaries.

Not spark, not fire, not heart.

Tonight, I sleep a little emptier.

Not because I lost a cube – but because I lost a part of myself.

And I don't know if I'll ever find the courage to twist it back together.

Dairy of a random person

Dear Diary,

I wonder how big the world is...

Because for me, it ends at the gate of my house.

I've never gone to the store alone.

Never take a walk by myself.

Never sat in a park just to feel the sun on my skin.

Why?

Because I'm a girl.

They say, "It's not safe."

But when will the world ever be safe if no one lets girls live in it?

Every time I ask, they tell me all the bad things that could happen.

As if I don't already know.

As if fear hasn't already been stitched into every corner of my mind since I was little.

My phone wallpaper is a sky – a fake freedom.

I dress up to go nowhere.

My dreams are scheduled between walls, chores, and silence.

My brother came back from a movie with friends tonight.

I stayed home. Again.

He doesn’t even ask anymore – because everyone already knows the answer when it comes to me: “No. Not alone.”

What hurts the most isn't the rejection.

It's the assumption that I don't need space.

That I'm not even meant to have it.

I’m not asking to disappear.

I’m asking to exist. Freely.

Even just for a few minutes.

I dream to..

To walk.

To breathe.

To live – without someone watching, judging, or dragging me back inside.

How long does a girl have to wait before she's trusted with her footsteps?

Maybe tomorrow will be different.

Maybe not.

But tonight, the only place I get to go – on this page.

Dairy of an unknown

Dear Diary, date wasn't mentioned

I don't even know why I'm writing this.

Maybe because these pages are the only ones that ever listened.

My aunt always treats me as her servant and showers me with hard words

called me names like I was garbage lying in her house.

She said I was a burden – a useless girl no one wanted.

And I believed her.

Because my father... he stood there.

He looked at me – and did nothing.

No word.

No sign that he cared.

He just turned away. Like always.

I wanted to scream.

Not because she hurt me – but because he didn't care that she did. And if he cared he didn't show.

How do you keep breathing when even your blood leaves you to rot?

Do they not see how I flinch when someone raises their voice?

Do they not notice how I've stopped speaking altogether?

Do they not care that I've become a ghost in this house, silently breaking every day?

I stood at the edge of the terrace today.

Just for a second, the wind felt kinder than any human I've ever known.

But I couldn't jump.

Not because I was scared to die – but because I had further responsibility to my parents and my younger sister...

Someone would finally say,

"I see you. I'm sorry. Stay."

But no one came.

So here I am, with a pen instead of silence.

A page instead of peace.

I'm tired, Diary.

Tired of proving I deserve love.

Tired of screaming inside while smiling outside.

Tired of being the girl everyone forgets to protect.

If tomorrow never comes...

Just know, I tried. I tried.

Dairy of an unknown

Dear dairy 12th may

I don't remember the last time I laughed and meant it.

Not a polite smile.

Not a fake "I'm fine."

But a real, belly-deep laugh that made my heart feel light.

Maybe that's the scariest part –

I've forgotten what happiness feels like.

This house... it eats joy.

It crushes it beneath slammed doors,

accusations were thrown like knives,

and the constant tension that never leaves,

not even when the lights go off.

They argue over everything –

money, decisions, blame, even me.

Like I'm a burden. A mistake. A problem they never asked for.

And every fight takes something from me.

A little lighter.

A little more hope.

A little more of me.

I used to sing.

I used to write poems.

I used to dream.

Now I just stare at ceilings and wonder if this is all life will ever be –

a never-ending mess that I'm trapped in, without a choice, without a voice.

I don't talk about it with anyone anymore.

Because when I tried, they said,

"Everyone has problems."

As if pain becomes invalid when it's common.

But no one sees how deep it goes for me.

How I wake up dreading the day.

How even birthdays feel like just another 24 hours in a broken home.

How even food tastes empty now.

They've taken everything.

My comfort.

My peace.

My laughter.

Even the mirror doesn't reflect the same girl anymore.

Just a shadow... of someone who once had sparkles in her eyes.

I didn't choose this.

And I don't know how to escape it.

But I know this:

I'm tired of surviving.

I want to feel alive again.

Someday... I hope I find that version of me who still believes in happiness Because right now, she's gone.

sometimes for a teenager or person, it gets suffocating for a person to understand what happens around them,

of course, they seek love,

for trust, for happiness... but mostly that is not served to them, and as a result, that person starts feeling like there is no light in their life. Usually, people don't even realise what's happening to them until the end, and even if they do understand, the world changes around them again. It takes years back to heal and understand.

As a family, every person should try to understand and know what is going on in the lives of their kids. Instead of triggering them more.

"Create a safe side for them, and not a mystery."

dairy of some unknown

Dear dairy

Today... my body cried for rest.

But no one listened.

I was bleeding – heavily.

So much, I had to change my pad twice in just 30 minutes. I was bleeding so badly that for me standing for a minute was also getting difficult.

Every step felt like knives inside me.

Every breath a silent scream.

But still...

the broom found my hand.

The dishes waited for me.

The floor demanded to be swept.

The clothes needed folding.

And everyone pretended like nothing was wrong –

because I'm just the daughter.

I whispered once, "Can I lie down for a bit?"

They looked at me like I asked something so wrong,

My grandmother said, you won't be able to give this excuse to your in-laws better you complete your work without any excuse ....

like rest was some kind of sin. As if periods are just an excuse.

As if this pain doesn't matter because I was born as me – a girl.

I wanted to scream:

"Do you not see the blood? The cramps? The dizziness?"

But I swallowed it like I always do.

Because when you're a daughter, your pain must stay quiet.

Neat. Hidden. Convenient.

No one asked how I was.

No one offered help.

No one said, "It's okay to sit down, you're in pain."

And it broke me.

Not just physically – but emotionally.

How can love exist in a home where your suffering is invisible?

That day we had guests and no maids were available due to covid I had to clean six rooms of our house, parking, and kitchen.

And that was not enough I had to cook for at least sixteen people.

My mother was not available that day she went out of the station and my aunt just acted as if she was working with me but she was not...

I started working at 7 in the morning and continuously without lunch I was working till 4 in the afternoon. I ended up washing dishes and other utensils of sixteen people...

I'm tired of being strong when I shouldn't have to be.

I'm tired of bleeding in silence.

I'm tired of being treated like a servant just because I was born with a womb.

I'm not just a daughter.

I'm human.

And today... I deserved rest.

Although my body was not responding to me, I did households without a single word... although I paid so hard my family told me that you are not strong, you are not capable of taking responsibility for our households...

What else do you want me to do should I die....?

But I got pain.

And silence.

Diary of an unknown

Dear dairy

I was so unwell that day – my body felt like it was giving up on me. I was vomiting every ten minutes, my head spinning, my strength fading with each hour.

I was sweating, shaking, and barely able to stand. And yet, not a single person in this house looked at me with concern.

No one paused to ask if I needed help, if I wanted to rest if I was okay. I lay there in pain, fighting waves of nausea, holding back tears not just from the sickness but from how utterly invisible I felt. It's strange, isn't it?

How the people who live with you – your own family – can walk right past your suffering and act like it's nothing. But the moment they need water, clothes folded, or a chore done, suddenly they remember you exist. Suddenly you're expected to stand up, act normal, and be of use – no matter how sick you are.

That's the part that hurts the most. It's not just about being ill. It's the fact that even in that state, even when your body is crying for rest, no one offers comfort or kindness. They only see your hands, not your heart.

They don't notice the tears behind your eyes or the way you're breaking down slowly, day by day. I wasn't looking for a grand gesture. Just one soft word. One hand on my head. One moment of care.

But I got silence, demands, and cold indifference. It makes me wonder – what am I to them? A daughter? Or just someone who's only noticed when something needs to be done? My health, my pain, my exhaustion – it doesn't matter here. And that realization hurt more than anything else my body felt that day.

Because when the people you love the most don't even care that you're suffering...

You begin to forget what love is supposed to feel like.

Dairy of some unknown person

Dear dairy

There are days I sit quietly in my room, and I wonder what it feels like to be loved by your own family. Not the kind of love that only shows up when they want something, but real love – the kind that asks, "How was your day?" or "Are you okay?" But I've never known that kind of love.

In this house, I'm invisible until someone needs a glass of water, help in the kitchen, or some errand done. No one speaks to me unless it's to give me work or instructions. No one asks me if I'm tired, if something's wrong, or even if I need a break.

I move through this home like a shadow – present, but unnoticed. It's not that they hate me – they don't even feel enough to do that. It's worse... they simply don't care. There is no warmth, no concern, no emotional connection.

I'm not included in conversations, not asked about my opinions, and not even looked at unless I'm needed. And what hurts the most is that they don't even have a reason for it. I didn't make some huge mistakes or rebel against them.

I've always done what they asked – quietly, without complaint, hoping one day they'd see me, really see me. But they never do.

I've watched them laugh together, talk, make plans, and ask each other about their lives – and I just sit there, invisible in plain sight. I'm not treated like a daughter.

I'm treated like a machine that runs quietly in the background. I keep hoping one day they'll change, that someone will ask how I'm feeling, but I'm slowly realizing that day might never come.

And maybe what hurts more than anything is the silence – not just theirs, but the one growing inside me.

And I know somewhere that if I am no more, they won't care and if they will max for five days then it won't matter to them. The one where I've stopped trying to be seen, and started learning how to live without being loved.

Dairy of a girl

Dear dairy

The Day I Realized I Was Never Free

I don't think my parents have ever seen me as me.

Not as a soul, not as a daughter, not even as a human being

just something they own.

A thing. A responsibility. A name on paper.

They never ask what I want, never care how I feel.

They make decisions for me, speak over me, and live through me

as if I don't exist beyond their expectations.

They treat me like property they bought the day I was born.

I'm told what to wear, who to talk to, how to behave,

what to dream, what to become

not for my happiness,

but so, they can hold their heads high in front of others.

Everything is about them –

how I make them look,

how I must obey,

how I can never say “no” because “we gave you everything.”

But love isn’t ownership.

And I’m not a trophy.

I’m not a robot they programmed to fulfil their plans.

I’m not a puppet to smile when they want and stay silent when they’re ashamed.

I’m a person. I feel. I ache. I cry into my pillow every night wondering why my voice doesn’t matter.

Why every decision about my life is made without me?

Why do they call it “love” but it feels more like a cage?

Sometimes I wonder if I’ll ever break free –

not just from the rules,

but from the belief that I owe them my entire existence.

Because love should feel like freedom.

But all I’ve ever known... is control.

I never felt like home was my place,
I never saw the love for me,
I never know the last care for me.

All I see is a plant of expectations,
And the flowers of hope that I will be their best child.
They bloom me with their thoughts,
Of impressing others

And under their shadow,
I lost myself...
I lost my actual phase....

The unknown dairy

Dear Diary,

Every day, I wake up not knowing whether I'll be praised or punished – not based on how I feel, but on how perfect I appear.

My parents don't raise me with love; they raise me with fear as if I'm a statue they're carving – violently – into what they believe the world wants to see.

I am not a daughter to them, I'm a reflection of their reputation, a walking image they want to display in front of society to say, "Look, our daughter is the best." And if I ever fail to meet that image – even slightly – I pay the price.

I've been beaten for getting one mark less than expected, for forgetting something during housework, for speaking too softly, or too loudly, or for nothing at all.

Sometimes the beatings come without a word. Just silence. Just anger. And I stand there, trying not to cry, because crying makes it worse. They say it's for discipline, that they're making me stronger, sharper, better

. But all I feel is smaller, more broken, more afraid to exist. I carry bruises on my arms, my legs, and my heart. No one outside sees them. No one knows. To the world, I'm the perfect daughter – well-spoken, respectful, obedient, always doing what I'm told.

But what they don't see is the pain that's hiding just beneath my skin. The pain of a child who doesn't know what love without violence feels like. I wonder sometimes – is this how daughters are supposed to be treated? Is it normal to be terrified of the people who brought you into this world? They never ask me if I'm okay, never hold me when I'm scared, never comfort me when I cry quietly in the corner of my room. I'm not being raised – I'm being programmed. For their pride.

For their status. For their need to be admired by a world that doesn't know what happens behind these walls. And I'm tired. Tired of being hurt and then told it was for my good. Tired of being silenced with fear.

Tired of being a prisoner in the name of perfection. All I ever wanted was to be loved – not displayed, not moulded, not beaten – just loved, like a real daughter.

But in this house, love is a weapon. And I'm just the girl they use it on.

Diary of a Struggling Teen

Dear dairy

Today was the kind of day that I don't think I'll ever forget – not because something special happened, but because something inside me shattered in a way I don't know how to fix.

It was just another class, just another question, and I raised my hand, heart pounding, not because I was sure of the answer, but because I was trying to be brave.

I wanted to be noticed, not for doing something wrong, but for trying. But the moment I opened my mouth, my teacher's face changed – from mild interest to disgust – and before I even finished speaking, she interrupted me with a sharp, cruel voice that sliced through the room. "Do you even have a brain? Are you here to study or just to waste everyone's time?" The class burst into laughter like a wave crashing over me. I felt my entire body freeze like I had been thrown into a storm with no warning. I didn't know where to look

. My eyes stung, my heart pounded in my ears, and I tried to hold back the tears that were building up behind my silence. She didn't stop there – she kept going, comparing me to other students, calling me slow, careless, and lazy, as if every word wasn't another stone thrown at my already fragile self-worth. At that moment, I didn't feel like a student.

I didn't feel like a person. I felt small, stupid, humiliated. I stared at my desk the rest of the day, unable to speak, unable to look anyone in the eyes.

The laughter had stopped, and the lesson went on, but inside me, something had gone completely still – like a part of me had shut down. All I kept thinking was, why me? Why would she say something like that when she knows we're all just trying? I'm not perfect, I know that. I make mistakes, I forget things, but I try. And trying was supposed to be enough.

But now it feels like no matter how hard I try, it'll never be good enough – not for her, not for school, maybe not for anyone. When I got home, I didn't speak to anyone.

I didn't eat, didn't move, I just lay on my bed, replaying that moment over and over again, and each time it hurt a little more. It wasn't just embarrassment.

It was the feeling that someone ripped away the little confidence I had built and replaced it with shame.

She probably doesn't even remember what she said. But I'll carry it with me for a long time – maybe forever.

"Because sometimes, it's not fists that break you – it's word."

Dairy of a boy,
Dear dairy

They said I stole the money.
₹500 from Ayaan's bag.
I didn't even know he brought money.

But by the time I found out,
they had already gone to the teacher.
The teacher called my parents.
Told them what my "friends" said.

And just like that...
I became "the thief."

No questions.
No truth.
Just blame.

My parents didn't even ask me once.
Not even once.
They came to school looking furious.
Not worried, not confused...
just ready to punish.

"Why would you do this?"
"Have we not given you enough?"

"We are ashamed of you."

I tried to speak.
Tried to tell them it wasn't me.
Tried to hold back the tears.

But my voice didn't matter.
Their minds were already made.
Because if three friends said it,
it must be true, right?

They didn't believe me.
Not even for a second.

They slapped me at home.
Took my phone.
Didn't let me eat dinner.

But I didn't care about the food.
Or the punishment.
I cared that they didn't look into my eyes
and see their son begging to be believed.

Later that night, the truth came out.
Ayaan had dropped the money on the school bus.
The conductor found it.
He got it back.

And suddenly... everyone was quiet.
No one said sorry.
No one hugged me.
They just said,
"Be careful next time. These mistakes happen."

But it wasn't my mistake.
It was theirs.
For not trusting me.
For making me feel like a criminal
just because someone else pointed a finger.

And now I know...
they love the version of me that makes them proud.
Not the one who needs to be defended.

Unknown dairy

Dear dairy

I don't think they'd care if I died.
Honestly.
That thought has been sitting with me all day.
Heavy.
Loud.
Unshakable.

Because today, I didn't speak.
I didn't eat.
I didn't even come out of my room.
But no one asked.
No one knocked.
No one noticed.

I was hurting so bad.
Crying under the blanket.
Wishing someone – anyone – would ask,
"What's wrong?"
"Are you okay?"
"Do you need a hug?"

But all I heard were dishes clinking,
TV sounds,

and their usual voices...
like I didn't exist.

Sometimes I think I'm just a shadow in this house.
I could scream and no one would hear.
I could collapse and they'd step over me.

They say they love me.
But love shouldn't feel this empty.
Love shouldn't make you feel like
you're just taking up space.
Like your pain is an inconvenience.

I've imagined leaving.
Running away.
Or worse – just not being here anymore.

And a dark part of me whispers...
"They won't even notice."

And that's what hurts the most.
Not the silence.
Not the loneliness.
But the truth behind it.

I don't want gifts.
I don't want money.

I just want to matter.
To be seen.
To be loved like I'm real.

But in this house,
I'm just... breathing.
Not living.

And if I stopped breathing tomorrow,
I wonder how long it would take
for someone to care.

Dairy of a kind person

Dear dairy

Today was one of the most painful days of my life – not because I failed a test or got punished, but because someone insulted the two people, I love the most in this world, and I couldn't do anything to stop it.

My teacher, the one meant to guide and protect us, stood in front of the whole class and spoke about my parents in the most disrespectful way I've ever heard. She said they were poor, that they probably couldn't even afford proper meals, and she used such cheap, abusive words about them – as if poverty is something shameful.

As if struggling and working day and night to raise a child with dignity deserves to be mocked. Everyone laughed. My classmates joined in, repeating her words, some whispering jokes, some pointing at my clothes, at my old shoes, at the tiffin I bring. And I just sat there, frozen.

I didn't cry – not because I wasn't hurt, but because I was trying so hard not to break in front of them. My parents are not rich, but they are good people.

They wake up before sunrise, work harder than anyone I know, go without things so I don't have to, and they never complain. They've given me love, values, and strength – things no money could ever buy. But today, none of that mattered. Today, in that classroom, being poor was treated like a sin.

And what's worse is that this is what our society teaches the next generation – that respect is tied to wealth, that struggling is funny, that if your parents don't drive a car or wear branded clothes, they deserve to be laughed at. It shattered me.

Not because I'm ashamed of my parents – I'm not. I'm proud of them. But because they didn't deserve to be humiliated like that.

I walked home with my head down, not because I did something wrong, but because I couldn't protect their name when it mattered the most. And the people who are supposed to shape our minds are the ones filling it with poison. Today, I saw how cruel people can be.

But I also promised myself one thing – one day, I will make sure the world knows that my parents were never less.

That their struggle was strength, and their love was more valuable than anything money could ever buy.

Unknown dairy

dear dairy

Today I finally broke. I couldn't hold it in anymore. My teacher – the one who's supposed to guide us, support us, protect us – has turned into the very reason I fear going to school. She bullies me, not once or twice, but almost every day.

In front of the entire class, she picks on me, taunts me, and mocks my handwriting, my speed, my voice, and even the way I sit. Today, I made one small mistake in my answer – just one – and she called me names that still ring in my ears.

"You're slow," "You're good for nothing," "You'll never achieve anything." The whole class laughed, some even repeated her words, and I sat there holding back my tears as hard as I could. But the moment I stepped out of that classroom and found a quiet corner, I cried. A lot.

And not just because of her words, but because of how small and helpless she made me feel.

I kept asking myself what I had done to deserve this – why she singled me out, why she says such hurtful things, and why no one steps in to stop her.

Teachers are supposed to lift children, not break them down like this.

But every time she humiliates me, it chips away at whatever little confidence I have left. I feel scared to raise my hand, scared to even be noticed.

I've started doubting myself in everything, just because one adult – the one who should be teaching with kindness – chooses to use her power to shame instead.

I don't know how many more days like this I can take. I don't want to cry like this anymore. I just want to feel safe in a classroom, not like I'm sitting in front of a firing squad.

I wish someone would notice. I wish someone would care.

Dairy that touches my heart

Dear dairy

Today wasn't about failure. It was about comparison. Again.

I woke up with hope–just a little. I looked in the mirror and thought, "Maybe today I'll be seen for who I am." But society doesn't care about who you are. It only cares about what you are not.

Not as good-looking as the girl with the perfect skin?

Loser.

Not scoring as much as the topper whose parents can afford 3 tuitions?

Loser.

Not as extroverted as the guy who speaks English like a foreigner?

Loser.

Not earning as much, not wearing branded clothes, not in a relationship, not popular, not trending, not following, not fitting...

They compare your silence to someone else's confidence.

Your scars to someone else's filters.

Your struggles to someone else's highlight reel.

And then—they judge. Label. Laugh. Whisper. Or worse, ignore.

I tried showing them my little victories. Solving that problem alone. Being kind when I could've been cruel. Helping others even when no one helped me.

But society doesn't clap for inner strength. They want trophies, not resilience.

I've learned that in this game society plays, no matter how hard you try, they'll always move the goalpost.

They'll remind you of who's "ahead" of you.

They won't care about where you started from—just where you haven't reached yet.

I want to scream: I'm not in a race with anyone.

But they'll still hand me a medal that says "Disappointment."

And worst of all?

Sometimes I start believing them.

That maybe I am not enough.

But deep down, I still hope that one day...

Someone will see me.

Not compared. Not ranked. Just seen—as enough.

Until then, I'll write here.

Because this page doesn't compare me to anyone.

It just listens.

And that is not enough even parents compare their children at its end...

Dairy of unknown

Dear dairy

They say parents love unconditionally.

But what if their love comes with a measuring scale?

Today, once again, I was compared.

To my cousin.

To my neighbour.

To the kid next door who dances better, studies harder, speaks sharper, and somehow, lives in my parents' head as who I should be.

"Look at her marks."

"Why can't you be like him?"

"She wakes up early, she studies without us telling her."

"He respects his parents—you just argue."

Every word felt like a slap—without sound, without bruises, but painful enough to leave cracks inside.

Do they not see how hard I try?

That I also want them to be proud.

That behind every mistake, there's a fear of letting them down again?

When they compare me, they don't realize...?

They're not motivating me.

They're slowly teaching me to hate myself.

To believe I'm not enough as I am.

To fear love as something I have to earn—by being someone else.

Today I smiled less.

Today I stayed quieter.

Because how do you speak up, when your voice is always compared to someone louder, clearer, and "better"?

They broke my heart, not with anger—but with disappointment.

With the silence that says, "You're not who we hoped for."

I wish they knew...

I don't want to be like her.

I want to be me–and still be loved.

But maybe that's too much to ask in a house where love is given based on report cards and relatives' opinions.

So, tonight I cried softly.

Not because I failed–

But because I wasn't allowed to just be me.

Conclusion

As we close these pages, we do not close the wounds they carry. Every diary in this book is a whisper of pain, a scream for love, a silent prayer that someone – anyone – would listen. These were not just stories; they were truths. Raw. Broken. Unfiltered.

Behind each entry was a soul asking for a hand, not a solution. A hug, not advice. A moment of understanding, not judgment. They remind us that sometimes, the loudest cries are the ones never spoken aloud – written instead in trembling hands, in pages wet with tears.

But this book is not only about sadness. It is a mirror held up to society – exposing the cracks we often ignore. It's a call to be gentler, softer, more human.

If these diaries have done anything, let it be this:

To make you pause.

To make you feel.

To make you care.

Because healing begins when we're finally heard.

If u read these lines,

If they felt your heart,

if it made you cry & incase

its high time to respect every person,

its high time to make a positive society,

& It's time to understand every little sentiment of every soul near you.

As a person you have to realize every little thought.

A letter to every reader,

We don't realize the pain that we give maybe fortunately or unfortunately. We don't every story, we don't know every pain, we don't know the cries, and we weren't to support. As a society instead of being so harmful let's start being kind, kind to every belonging of this world, kind to every soul that exists. If you are a child, be kind and regardful to your parents and society, if you are a parent remember it should be always your child first before the words of society and finally to every person dear don't think so worst about others you know when it will return to you.

I request every reader to always know that we don't know how much they cried, we don't know what they suffered, we don't know how much their hearts bounced. If you see a happy face maybe you cannot see the pain behind that face, if you see a dull face maybe you haven't seen the crying face. Respect every person, if you can show a rose of empathy to them, and if that grows wish for a supportive and positive society.

I wish as a writer, and as a human in regard to humanity that together let's build a happy society that will understand every child and human. Which will bring the aroma of positivity and togetherness.

Dear Diary

"The end is just another beginning in disguise."

www.ingramcontent.com/pod-product-compliance
Lightning Source LLC
Chambersburg PA
CBHW050016170726
48282CB00025B/421
* 9 7 8 9 3 7 1 3 9 1 2 2 1 *